YellowBlack

Books by Haki R. Madhubuti

Poetry
Run Toward Fear: New Poems and A Poet's Handbook
HeartLove: Wedding and Love Poems
Ground Work: New and Selected Poems of Don L. Lee/
    Haki R. Madhubuti from 1966-1996
Killing Memory, Seeking Ancestors
Earthquakes and Sunrise Missions
Book of Life
Directionscore: New and Selected Poems
We Walk the Ways of the New World
Don't Cry, Scream
Black Pride
Think Black

Non-Fiction
Tough Notes: A Healing Call for Creating Exceptional Black Men
Claiming Earth: Race, Rage, Rape, Redemption: Blacks Seeking a
    Culture of Enlightened Empowerment
Dynamite Voices: Black Poets of the 1960s
Black Men: Obsolete, Single, Dangerous? The Afrikan American
    Family in Transition
From Plan to Planet: Life Studies; The Need for Afrikan Minds and
    Institutions
Enemies: The Clash of Nations
A Capsule Course in Black Poetry (co-author)
African Centered Education (co-author)
Kwanzaa: A Progressive and Uplifting African American
    Holiday

Anthologies
Releasing the Spirit: A Collection of Literary Works from Gallery 37
    (co-editor)
Describe the Moment: A Collection of Literary Works from
    Gallery 37 (co-editor)
Million Man March/Day of Absence:
    A Commemorative Anthology (co-editor)
Confusion by any Other Name: Essays Exploring the Negative
    Impact of "The Black Man's Guide to Understanding the Black
    Woman" (editor)
Why L.A. Happened: Implications of the "92 Los Angeles
    Rebellion (editor)
Say that the River Turns: The Impact of Gwendolyn Brooks (editor)
To Gwen, With Love (co-editor)

YellowBlack

THE FIRST TWENTY-ONE
YEARS OF A POET'S LIFE

A MEMOIR

HAKI R. MADHUBUTI

THIRD WORLD PRESS
Chicago

Third World Press
Publishers since 1967

First Edition
Printed in the United States of America
Book design by Denise Borel Billups
Author Photograph by Lynda Koolish
Photograph insets from Author's personal archives

Library of Congress Cataloging-in-Publication Data

Madhubuti, Haki R., 1942-
  YellowBlack : the first twenty-one years of a poet's life:
a memoir
/ Haki R. Madhubuti.—1st ed.
    p. cm.
  ISBN 0-88378-261-8 (hardcover : alk. paper)
 1. Madhubuti, Haki R., 1942—Childhood and youth.
 2. Poets,
American—20th century—Biography. 3. African
American poets—Biography. I.
Title: Yellow Black. II. Title.
  PS3563.A3397Z478 2005
  813'.54—dc22
                                          2005014359

10 09 08 07 06 05 6 5 4 3 2 1

Owo foro adobe (snake climbing the palm)
Performing the unusual or the impossible.

For my children,
my sister's children,
my sister Jacklyn,
and
young people of all nations
the real hope for the world

In Memory of

Helen Maxine Graves Lee
Gwendolyn Brooks
Fannie Lou Hamer
Ossie Davis
Calvin C. Hernton
Robert S. Browne
Jeff R. Donaldson
Ray Charles
James Forman
John H. Johnson
Edward W. Said
Barbara A. Sizemore
Czeslaw Milosz
Ron Milner
Vernon Jarrett
Lu Palmer
Steve Neal
Penny (Aunt Sis) Nicholson
Jack Newfield
Susan Sontag
Iris Chang
Oscar Brown Jr.
Lorenzo Thomas
and
James (Jimmy) Lee

ACKNOWLEDGEMENTS

I would like to thank Rose Perkins for translating my legal pad language into readable text; Gwendolyn Mitchell and Quraysh Ali Lansana for their editing and especially to Ms. Mitchell for her logical and expert reordering of my text; to my first readers, Pamela York, Diane Turner, Regina Jennings, Willalyn Fox, Jacqueline Imani Bryant, Bakari Kitwana, Delores Lipscomb, Murry DePillars and Bennett Johnson; and to Denise Borel Billups for her fine design. I would like to give thanks to Walter Lomax for keeping the wolves off my back as I was writing *YellowBlack*.

Contents

CONTENTS

CONTENTS

Prologue

Yes

I have nothing of my mother's
but memories
I have no piece of cloth,
nor any re-read books,
no recipes for spaghetti,
cakes or coleslaw.
There are no photographs of the two of us
laughing or holding hands,
I don't even remember the
beauty of her voice.
All I have deep inside of me are her last
words, "you are smarter than us Don,
use the library, take care of your
sister and learn from what I have done
wrong."

I often tell audiences that I grew up around pimps and ho's slamming Cadillac doors on the streets of Detroit's Blackbottom and Chicago's Westside. I was dropped into a culture of Black inferiority and white answers. I became a man at twelve years old and the music of Motown, Miles Davis and Louis Armstrong helped to save me and introduced me to deep breathing, discipline and the many mysterious worlds of the trumpet. I watched my mother live and die trying desperately to navigate our lives in a culture of survival, dependency and deep poverty. I was born into Black music and discovered Black literature at fourteen and my life experienced a profound reversal that required learned answers from my avalanche of questions about Black existence and ignorance.

My sister and only sibling had her first child at fourteen, gave birth to six children before the age of twenty-seven and never married. I remained outside of her choices and pleasures and discovered that insight is non-discriminating if one has a searching attitude toward life. I chose poetry, music and visual art as lifelines and quickly matured in the U.S. Army, Black struggle, the Black Arts Movement, institution building and the Human Rights work of the sixties and beyond.

I graduated into academics, marriage, children and Black institution-development in the seventies. I gave up minor fame as Don L. Lee and became Haki R. Madhubuti, a brother with a last name who few learned to pronounce. I continued to search and work for authenticity, integrity, a writing voice, beauty, and a way of winning the many cultural, racial, economic and political wars. I fought hard to stay honest and productive as a poet and activist.

I sought an artful response to the penetrating and redefining cultures of White Supremacy and Nationalism, celebrity-hood, money, sex, corporate greed, the destructive incarceration of young black and brown boys and men, and a compromised leadership, Black and white, who prostitutes themselves in the name of Jesus like used razor blades, to justify their lies, cowardice and corrupt lifestyles.

I realized early that independent economic development for most Black folks is highly restrictive and mainly limited to the ministry, undertaking, hair business, the Black sex trade (pimps and ho's), the underground economy of drugs, gambling, and the sale of any items we acquire or liberate and pass on at substantial savings to our community. I also realized that Democracy is a code word to confuse the poorly educated majority as the white-monied few continue to run this country like a private club. I learned quickly, around the age of eleven, that religion in America not only dominates the way we think and act, but presents a future and after-world that only made sense to babies, children and people who refuse to think and question reality. I lost my adopted cultural mother, Gwendolyn Brooks, in December of the first year of the new century. Her loss inspired me to continue to sharpen the meaning of my adopted name: just, precise, accurate and dependable.

YellowBlack is about my birth mother, Helen Maxine Graves Lee, her children Don Luther Lee and Jacklyn Lee, and the world that claimed us. To some it is America's same old horror story. For me it is the first twenty-one years that shaped and prepared me for the life of a poet, writer, activist, publisher, editor, educator, husband, father, institution builder and Black man.

This story has been eating at my heart for

over forty years. After a serious fall off of my Bianchi Limited bicycle at about 26 miles an hour, which tore up my right leg, I knew while walking home that it was time to write. I kept a journal and a shoebox full of notes and during the summer of 2003 was motivated by my father's death to begin writing in earnest.

The style of *YellowBlack* is a mixture of prose, prose poetry, free verse and street riffs. These short sketches make up a young life that is only one story in a nation that is still trying to find its heart and soul as it makes up its mind about the necessity and beauty of African Americans, Black people, in our journey to adulthood, empowerment, peace and some precious moments of joy.

PART ONE
YellowBlack

1942

I am told that I was born on a night
when sun and moon fought for recognition.
My father played five-stud-poker with men who
did not like him, while two midwives gently
opened my mother's legs so I could slide
headfirst into a world not ready for complicated
questions or uncommon ideas from people with
the deepest of color, Black.
The year was 1942.

Up North, the United States Justice
Department threatened 20 editors of Black
newspapers with sedition charges for exposing
segregation and injustice in the U.S. military;
John H. Johnson begins publishing his first
magazine *Negro Digest* and Margaret Walker's
first book of poetry, *For My People* is published
and she becomes the first Black poet to be
featured in Yale University's series of younger
poets.

Up North, W.E.B. DuBois, Paul Robeson,
Duke Elllington, A. Philip Randolph, Ida B.
Wells and others were busy laying the ground-
work for my entry.

However, in Little Rock, Arkansas on February
23, 1942 I was one of hundreds of babies
getting used to warm milk from a mother's
breast, unaware of the massive storms,
hurricanes and volcanoes awaiting us.

A world offering fire, not milk or comfort,
a world unaware of a generation making ready
to question whiteness and separate water
fountains.

Don Luther Lee

I was not given my father's name, James (Jimmy) Lee. He was not present at my birth and my mother threw darts at a generic name sheet and Don fell off the page. To this day I do not know the meaning or origin of Don or Lee. I do not know if Lee is European or Asian or if my parents were really married or loved each other. I do know that my mother clutched me close to her heart and seldom let me go, especially on our trips north, where frequent hunger pains were a fact of our existence. I didn't know that her life would be short and full of vacancies and violence. This only meant that my introduction to pure evil and poverty would be early, in abundance and life-defining until thinking preceded actions, reactions and people telling me "you are not Black enough."

Being not "Black" enough would follow me all
of my life. However, it was during my young
life that color and the texture of my hair were
most troubling and life determining. Light
skinned or fair skinned Black folks were
considered the benefactors, materially and
culturally, because they are the closest to
the hue of white people. If being one half, one
third, or one forth white was a benefit, I am
here to dispel that myth. My life has been that
of an outsider and if it weren't for Black music
and literature I would probably be sitting in
some prison or fertilizing the weeds growing
from the earth covering my body. The only
guarantee I had as a young boy growing up in
urban America was that there was always
another fight waiting.

Jimmy Lee: One

My father was a fast question.

He cared greatly about himself.

It was not that my mother and I were after-
thoughts, it was that to think about us and our
well-being took him away from the important
matters that occupied the space of a player-hus-
tler, himself. Feeling superior, he never wanted
to work for white people.

This feeling was partially based upon the fact
that the great majority of them with whom he
was in contact could never get his name right,
kept calling him boy and sometimes nigger Jim.
To him this insult was worse than spit in the
face in ninety-degree heat.

In the community on our side of the tracks,
Jimmy Lee was known as a "bad nigger."
People who did not know him knew of him and
also knew that he had to leave Little Rock,
Arkansas, soon.

Little Rock

Mostly what I remember about Little Rock was that the city and the people were unkind to us.

We were forced into back doors, unclean toilets and water fountains. Saleswomen took our money with gloved hands. We occupied the balconies of local movie houses that charged us downstairs prices to often see ourselves portrayed as buffoons, gofers, big-eyed tap dancers and musicians.

Most whites called us nigger as if nigger was our name and permanently stamped on our foreheads. It was not uncommon during the darkness of a Saturday matinee for many of the big boys to relieve themselves from the balconies choosing to pee onto the main floor in public rather than accept the disrespect and filth of "Negro Only" restrooms. This was one of my first lessons in Black resistance and civil disobedience.

The World As We Knew It

We were innocent property. We did not know
the history of white men in robes with Bibles or
in uniforms with guns and lies.

We never discussed the genocide of Native
Americans, did not know the recent history of
Jews and their many death marches, had no idea
of how we came to this land. All life was con-
temporary and a long day's work.

The Middle Passage was simply a section from a
song or a part of a Paul Laurence Dunbar
poem. History was not forgotten because it was
not known. Our ignorance was contagious,
large and confining.

White Supremacy and Nationalism had
convinced most of us we were the problem.

We were never consumed by big ideas. We were always on the periphery of our own existence. Our discussions were limited to food, housing, clothing, work, weekends, pleasure and money-less-ness. We on instinct sought pleasure and the material toys of our class. Modern enslavement works best when the enslaved do not realize the magnitude and mechanics of slavery as well as their own contribution to their condition.

Our station in life demanded that we accept an "education" that never, and I do mean never, taught us or allowed and encouraged the investigation of liberating ideas or even allowed us to question the reality of our own wretched existence. Seldom, in my family were questions raised beyond the front pages and sometimes the interiors of daily newspapers. The act of serious, continuous life-long study as a tool for

self-liberation and knowledge acquisition was
about as foreign as yearly vacations. Most
certainly self-definition, which is central to any
level of empowerment, seldom got in the way of
seeking the basic necessities of life. This limiting
of practical or theoretical knowledge worked,
because it kept us at each other's throats, as in
blaming the victim for our condition as if we
had the power or resources to make substantial
changes. Thus, the literature (mainly newspapers
and on occasion magazines) that we consumed
always confirmed in the language of the day the
rightness and depending upon medium, the
righteousness of the assessment.

The fighting history of David Walker, Sojourner
Truth, William Wells Brown, Frederick
Douglass, Marcus Garvey, W.E.B. DuBois, Ida
B. Wells-Barnett, Carter G.Woodson, J.A.
Rodgers, James Weldon Johnson and countless

others wrote, published, organized, struggled
and literally fought their way into the consciousness of America but seldom entered our world.

We never even cared to understand what was
happening to us. There was a shared past;
however, we had no knowledge of it. We
survived in urban areas by avoiding confrontation
with those persons outside our communities
unless backed to the wall with no other option.
We clearly had examples in our past but were not
aware of their brave words and work, with the
possible exception of Marcus Garvey and his
Universal Negro Improvement Association
(UNIA).

Sad to say, love, death and deep memory
seldom brought new insights, only simple joy or
pain. The cobwebs of our minds were effective
and difficult to cut through.

The Book

The only book in our home was the family
Bible. A big white, leather covered Bible,
bought from a white door-to-door salesman
who smiled a lot and called my grandmomma
sister. This is what I was told by my mother
who had me at fifteen and like most Black
people of the south, was nurtured to live in the
Black church. Religion was the first and last
answer in our home.

Most of us had a minister in the family.
My paternal grandfather preached in storefront
churches all his life. The only book we could
read without interruption was the Bible,
everything else had a double why to it.

"In Our House, There was God"

In our house Jesus was never an afterthought, he preceded eating, sleeping and playing the numbers.

I came from a long line of southern storefront preachers, all very Black, the color of coal and dark chocolate mixed with licorice.

The Bible was salvation and tomorrow on earth. The men among us loved their women the color of peach-vanilla. In our home women covered their bodies three times: once with clothes, second with scripture and third with men.

My mother would often talk to herself about the hypocrisy of the Word and the Word interpreters. Her life was to be the perfect metaphor of words not working and the word interpreters forever trying to get some.

Fear

I grew up in a culture of fear. We lived in
unadulterated terror where white men in white
sheets and suits quoted from the Christian Bible
as they lynched the strength out of our people
and expected us to remain mute—"see no evil,
speak no evil and hear no evil"—only to endure
evil, and smile. We lived in evil's way. We did not
understand that the ultimate rulership would be
white men in Black robes and suits populating
courts and corporate boardrooms throughout
the land. They passed laws that legalized Black
ignorance, fear and existence. They created a
commercial culture that captured the minds of
babies before birth. This is not recent history.
The fact that over a million Black and Brown
men would eventually populate the prisons of
this land, and that buying and buying, shopping
and shopping would emerge as therapy and
entertainment has little to do with genetics,
biology or Black culture.

The First Poet

Our mother sometimes shared stories with my sister and me. A glimpse into long ago. It was her way of saying life was not always like this for me and it won't always be like this for you. I remember how she'd retell events in vivid detail. I didn't know it then, but I feel she was giving me permission to take her memories and make them mine.

One Sunday afternoon a poet came to town. He was mellow-yellow and spoke in a high sounding voice. He read his poems in a local Black church, where the preacher was considered progressive, and read other books along with the Bible.

He was the only man in our community with a college education, majoring in Theology at Howard University. He returned to Little Rock because a woman the color of rich earth stole his heart and wouldn't give it back.

This was my first reference to the poet named
Langston Hughes. This soon-to-be-famous and
progressive poet came to our town. The poet
who was forced to testify before the House on
Un-American Activities where he lost part of his
soul. He never forgot who he was, lived in
Harlem most of his life, started thousands of
Black folks to think lovingly and creatively
about themselves. He wrote poems and prose
that would challenge the discourse of this land.

Jacklyn Ann

My sister was born in Ecorse, Michigan,
a factory town outside of Detroit.

We arrived in the night with hope, smiles and
high expectations just before her birth in
September of 1943. We left six months later
running (an early symbol of a life becoming),
my father had gambled all the food, furniture
and rent money away and men were looking for
him. We landed in Inkster, Michigan another
appendage of Detroit for a minute and ended
up on Detroit's' lower east side, Black Bottom.
My father disappeared two months later, stating
that my sister was not his child.

This was like a razor cut in the body of my
mother, a seventeen-year-old girl who had only
known one man. My mother, a woman with
little education, extraordinary good looks, a
great body, southern smile, light skin with long

straight Black hair, the beauty that could turn the heads of blind men. She was left with two children under the age of four, the stars didn't shine that night and it was the first, but not the last time there was real fear in my mother's eyes. It was also the last time she cried over a man.

Maxine and Jimmy Lee

My mother loved my father.

He took her virginity and gave her me.

Her love for him was life-changing and life-determining. She never loved again.

She said it was too painful.

Her beauty attracted oceans of men from all cultures. Few men could really handle the way she looked. Men of wealth, influence and potential proposed to her.

She never married again.

She said that love is a beautiful concept but not for women like her. Men wanted to lock up her beauty. They did not trust themselves and refused to trust her. She said the hearts of most men were corrupted in the act of becoming men. She chose to be alone with her children and memories of southern sunlight.

It was clear to her, no one was going to take care of us, but us.

The Roads Between

We escaped the "white only" signs and
name calling of the South.
We ate fried chicken with hot sauce,
riding the rear seats of Greyhound buses leaving
in the night on the local from Little Rock via
Memphis by way of Indianapolis and fifteen
other stops that had no meaning to us other
than "don't get off here."
This was before washrooms on buses.
We had to hold our pee (after we filled the
emergency jelly jars) until momma felt it safe
and civil in places where "Negro" rather than
nigger was the accepted ethnic name of our
people. She didn't want us to get too used to
other people's ignorance.

Detroit

We lived in a building on the east side of Detroit owned by Reverend Wright, the minister of one of the largest Black churches in the city.

My mother was the janitor and his "outside" woman. He wore dark suits, drove a big Cadillac and always talked about himself. I'll never forget watching my mother carry garbage cans from a four-story, twelve-flat building twice a week. When she mopped the front stairs and entranceway, my sister and I would do the dusting. I was ten, Jackie was eight and my mother at twenty-five, after a series of unfulfilling jobs, visited Rev. Wright's church.

We moved into his building's basement apartment the same week. God worked his magic. Rev. Wright would visit twice a week, Monday and Thursday afternoons, and insisted that my mother not come back to his church. At the time I didn't understand those instructions. It was only a year later that I looked up the word used most often on the streets to describe most ministers, hypocrites. By then I was shining shoes, bagging groceries and saving most of my nickels and dimes for an unknown future. I had tasted hunger and knew at a very young age that I had to work if we were to eat.

Rev. Wright was a kind man, in his fifties, large and very Black. He had worker's hands, a Paul Robeson voice and a big smile. Fourteen months after this arrangement, Rev. Wright was killed. He reportedly fell off the platform at the National Baptist Convention, where he was running for the president. Less than a week after his burial, his wife put us out of the basement apartment we occupied.

Out of complete desperation, with no family to speak of and few genuine friends, my mother and the streets took to one other.

Jimmy Lee: Two

My father never lowered his head; however, his
soul had been bastardized by people who
thought him less than the animals they ate.
The only way to prove to himself and them
that they were wrong was to leave Little Rock,
and earn the only thing they respected, money.
He visited Little Rock yearly in a new Cadillac
wearing three hundred dollar suits.

He would systematically fuck their wives and
daughters. This went on for about ten years
when he realized that, indeed his soul had been
stolen.

He never went South again and white women
ceased to be a challenge for him, too many
Black women were willing to take care of him
and he knew that southern "justice" was only
the next trip away.

His Eight F's of women containment and control
guided his life: find them, feed them, fool them,
foreplay them, fuck them, forget them, find
another, fast.

When the women, children and old men went
to church, my father was not among them. I do
not know if he ever set foot on sacred ground. I
do not know if he prayed, meditated, spoke in
tongues, whispered holy words to himself in times
of stress, or felt empathy for the teachings of holy
men and women. I do know that he loved Black
women and music—equally, passionately and
often.

This love of women would rule his life and Black
music was internal food for his soul. He played at
the trombone. J.J. Johnson's photographs along

with those of Louis Armstrong, Charlie Parker and Count Basie populated his private spaces.

He changed women like he changed clothes. He said that the only thing more satisfying than the music of Duke Ellington was a young dark skinned woman's fresh pussy.

Street Lesson: One

I saw my first killing at twelve in an after-hours
joint I cleaned to help make ends meet.
Two men were arguing at the bar:
one, very strong and domineering;
the second very feminine—almost woman-like,
what we called at that time a "sissy" or "faggot."
The domineering man suddenly hit the woman-
like-man and knocked him to the floor.
He slowly rose from the floor fumbling at his
purse and upon rising he began to slap his attacker
like a woman fighting another woman.
With each slap, the man-like-man grabs his
throat and face, trying desperately to hold back
the gushing blood and loose skin jumping off his
body. The woman-like-man had razor blades
between his fingers. As the man-like-man went
down with eyes of disbelief and horror,
the woman-like-man calmly walked away
stating, "You musta not had a mamma, bitch."

Men loving women was etched into our Black souls. We were instructed by our grandmothers to love only one woman at a time but most of us didn't believe it.

Maxine

My mother was the color of papaya and
bananas, her smile could weaken the strongest
of men. She was uncommonly beautiful.
Her face and body forced men to forget so
called social etiquette. They all, upon seeing
her, would dream for a moment.

Many men, married, single and committed,
old, young, saints, sinners and in-between
wanted a chance with Helen Maxine Graves.
Most men were willing to risk everything to
taste the flesh of a fourteen year old girl in a
woman's body who had no idea that her beauty
would define her life and that of her children.
Jimmy Lee got the first hit, with his smile,
music, lies, sexual know-how and promises.
She ceased looking at other boys or men.
This was her first mistake.

Jimmy Lee: Three

Black Detroit was a southern midwestern city.
Negroes encouraged by the *Michigan Chronicle*
and the *Chicago Defender* migrated North in
masses looking for anything better than working
sunup to sundown for people who hated them
and with no hope or history of owning
anything, not even their minds.

Jimmy Lee saw opportunity and grabbed it like
feet to freedom and evening meals. I've never
known him to work for white folks. He said
once you start, it becomes contagious. He had a
smile that could sell dirt to housewives, and a
rap that could steal cream from coffee.

On the legit side he sold used and new furniture
in his storefront during the day and after hours
ran a gambling house and a policy wheel in the
rear of the store. He wore his money tied in
rubber bands with hundreds and fifty dollar bills

facing the public. He was show. Always clean, always looking for an angle. There was no such thing as lies or truth. His motto was, say anything that works. He spent the first seventy years of his life raising hell and the last ten trying not to go there. I'm sure he failed. But, then again he may be talking trash to God.

Don

I started from raw earth.

What was given came from the state

in the form of uneatable cheese and a bad

education delivered by white teachers who, for

the most part, viewed their time in Negro

schools as punishment or missionary work.

I did not receive anything material or memo-

rable from my father, grandfather, grandmother,

most aunts and uncles.

My mother introduced me to the Detroit Public

Library, encouraged me to master the trumpet,

pointed me to works of Richard Wright and

Chester Himes.

She often said that she loved me and my sister.

She declared me intelligent and smart and said

I should look after my sister.

She said that my sister was too much like her:

European-pretty with long, straight, black hair,

street-fast, high-yellow color with an unforgiv-

ing body and fucking too early.

She said dark-skinned Black men would misuse her because they hated themselves and that she and Jackie were the closest women they could get to white women and not get killed.

She was right. Children often duplicate a mother's personal history.

My mother worked hard to make ends meet for my sister and me. Even though our material lives were impoverished, my life began to change when I was introduced to other worlds. On my birthday, one year, my mother took me to a five-and-dime store to purchase a gift. She bought me a blue plastic airplane with blue wheels, a blue propeller, and a blue string on the front. When I took it home, I rolled it on the linoleum floor. I was happy to get that airplane. Then, the following week she took my sister and me to Dearborn, Michigan, where she

occasionally did domestic day work. This was
back when most of our mothers who worked
outside the home cleaned up white folks'
homes. Dearborn was where the men who ran
the automobile industry lived. I quickly noticed
that they lived differently.

There were no five-and-dime stores in Dearborn
at that time. There were craft shops. There were
hobby shops where white mothers and fathers
bought their children airplanes in boxes. In the
boxes were wooden parts and directions for
assembling and gluing small airplanes. It might
take a day or two or a week or so for the son
generally, but sometimes the daughter, to
assemble a plane.

If the child needed help, the father would sit
down and assist in putting the plane together,
and guess what? After the assembling of the

plane, the little boy did not roll it on the floor like I did. He took it outside and flew it in the air.

Do you see my point? In this small slice of life, there are two different types of consciousness being developed. In my case and that of other poor youth, we would buy the plane already assembled; take it home, and hope that it rolled on the floor like a car or a truck. But it was an airplane! In Dearborn, the family would invest in a learning toy that the child would put together, and through this process learn work ethics, science, and mathematics. As a result of that labor, the plane would fly. I was learning to be a consumer who depended upon others to build the plane for me. The child in Dearborn worked on his plane, made a financial and emotional investment, and through his labor and brainpower produced a plane that flew.

Translating that into the larger world, I was being taught to buy things and to use my body from the neck down, while the white middle class and upper-class boys were taught very early to prepare themselves to build and run things, and to use their brains. Two different worlds. My world depended upon others and on working for others. Their world consisted of controlling, running, making things, and having other people work with and someday for them.

People of African ancestry are caught between a hurricane and a volcano when it comes to the acquisition of life-giving and life-sustaining knowledge. Too many of our children are trapped in urban school systems, which have been programmed for failure. And all too often the answers to what must be done to correct this injustice are left in the hands of those most

responsible for creating the problem. I could
not articulate the problem at such a young age,
but the questions of our material and cultural
conditions was beginning to eat at my soul.

My mother was caught in this trap of few
opportunities, lack of preparation, a perpetual
feeling of failure and knowing that all the men
in her life only wanted sex and to own her.
They wanted her to love them, but reciprocat-
ing was not in the cards at the level she felt
necessary for her to say yes and mean it.

Quietly, and without much discussion with me
or my sister, she decided to use the one quality
about her that was, without a doubt, superior to
most others: her beauty and body.

I fought and studied my way through public schools without my mother ever meeting any of my teachers. She never visited any of my schools after registration. There were eight of them in Detroit and Chicago. The education of her children was relegated to telling us how smart we were and the importance of libraries.

Between nightlife, highs, bouts of depression, and embarrassment, she read books that never seemed to help her. I was her go-for and the public library became a second home, more stable and nurturing than the apartments we moved to every year.

As an urban nomad, I learned the streets of Detroit and Chicago. The Greyhound bus served as primary carrier between cities for us and other poor travelers who seldom smiled or shared stories.

It was clear that we all knew each other's name.
I wanted quiet in my life more than love. I had
tired of noise. The noise of public school, the
parties of never ending weekends, the hurt and
confusion of verbal and physical fights that
closed most days and most of all, the noise
in my own head that had few answers for the
angry, debilitating confusion of a non-
functioning family always in need, always on
the verge of collapsing.

Camden, Arkansas

Summers were memorable days and nights in Camden, Arkansas. Summers were also relief, smiles and safety.

Most of our kin were welcoming and instructive. We shucked corn with hands used to cold and gloves, ate yellow skinned watermelon, greenbeans and yams from fields where we wore red dirt between our toes.

We dodged spiders and nameless bugs in outdoor toilets remembering to pee and do number two before sundown.

In Camden, chickens were freshly killed, pigs cured and fish jumped onto our hooks. We played without fear. After front porch baths in metal tubs on hot nights, we slept four to a bed as our summers flashed before us and the Greyhound waited for the fading smiles of two street kids returning tearfully to the coming snow and dangers of Detroit and Chicago.

We did not play hockey,

most of us could not swim too well.

This had nothing to do with genes or biology.

There were no organized sports in my young life. We

were warm weather people.

Our bones tied to the sun.

The South and North of my time said no

to our using their pools, ponds, and rivers and fields

for recreation.

This is one reason for our gravitation toward basket-

ball, baseball and football.

We learned to outrun the wind, shoot the eye out of

milk crates, out jump the sky and catch a football in

one hand running full speed in a fog.

Those sports were cheap and we didn't have to ask

permission.

Grandfather Graves

My grandfather on my
mother's side was a rolling stone.
The rumor was that he had children in every
state of the union except Alaska, Hawaii, South
Dakota, North Dakota and Utah.
The Graves men attracted women
like they were perfume in gift boxes wrapped in
got-cha tape. I've never known him to work.
My grandmother did, every day.
Our grandmother, not our mother's mother,
was the third or fourth common-law wife of our
grandfather. Anger wore her face like an iron
mask. It may have been because we,
my sister and I, were not blood kin.
Every time we visited Camden, Arkansas
our grandfather left on another of his many
trips. She took his absences out on us.
We still wear the scars.

Johnny Graves

Johnny Graves was a pretty man.
He served in World War II and
in uniform there was not a woman
on earth who could say no.
He, my mother's only full-blooded brother
(as mentioned earlier, half-brothers and sisters
populated the land).
Uncle Johnny had a smile and a way
that endeared him to my sister and me.
Behind that smile was a heart of dried stones.
Within his eyes were lies upon double lies.
His heart, it was said, was the dust of burnt coal.
He went through women with the
speed of Negroes consuming free Johnny Walker
Red; if he wanted it, he could talk a baby off
his/her mother's breast.
Uncle Johnny was small in stature,
muscled enough to look good in t-shirts.
He thought himself bad.

He carefully picked his fights,

mainly with women. One day, hot and slow,

he exchanged words in public with a man small-

er than himself.

They took it to the back yard. Unknown to

Uncle Johnny, the man was a former Marine.

The stranger methodically took

Johnny Graves apart

paying particular attention to his face.

After he healed he had to leave Detroit.

In Chicago, he continued to walk the streets,

frequenting the best night spots,

run his women and tell me how bad he was,

as if I didn't have a memory.

Aunt Mayme

Aunt Mayme filled spaces that only a sister
could hear. There was this distant desert a half
century away, on the negro door to "Jewtown"
at Chicago's 14th and Hastings, a one-house
street with a broom factory on the corner,
There stood a home, with walk over stairs con-
necting sidewalk to hope, where summers and
other drop-off times were spent with a loving
aunt, many children and an uncle larger than
doorways named Jesse James. He wore guns,
had a majestic smile on a large bald head. He
adored his family and worked all the time.

Our days were spent collecting metal and
saleable junk in secure alleys where work was
not begging for jobs but inventing employment,
making do with ideas and nothing. Knowing
that if everything is everything, then nothing is
nothing.

Except we, my sister and I, had Aunt Mayme
for precious moments with Uncle Jesse who
worked all the time.

During summers and some autumns at irregular
drop-offs, my sister and I received love
uncommon, full meals and deep warmth. We
learned the location of family from Aunt
Mayme, a host of first cousins and that giant of
a black man with guns, a winning and intelligent smile, Jack Johnson-bold baldhead with
promises and safety in his eyes.

Music

My young life was absent of smiles. The only people I looked up to were Black musicians. Miles Davis was my man—always clean—he set the style for the young men with his hard dark bop-look. His sound was sweet enticement to women and they gravitated toward him like a "free shoe store." I wanted to play me some trumpet.

The Italian band leader at my middle school said that I was too skinny and didn't have the wind for the trumpet. Welcome to racism pre-high school. On the way home, I stopped at the poor men's bank, the neighborhood pawn shop, to inquire about the used trumpets in the window. The cheapest one was thirty-three dollars, a small fortune for a boy barely making $2.50 in a good week.

The white-Jewish pawn shop owner was a musician and could see in my eyes what he called "deep determination." He made me a deal, three dollars down, a dollar a week that included private trumpet lessons. I ran home, robbed my savings bank, went back with four dollars and started lessons that Friday afternoon in May of 1955.

A professional musician, he worked with me all summer. He loved Black music and taught me not only the trumpet but rules for survival and talked fondly about the lives of the local Black musicians. By the end of the summer I was ready. I returned to school, trumpet in hand, went to band rehearsal and auditioned. I easily became first trumpet and proved to the band leader and myself that if I really wanted something, "no" was not an option and failure was a foreign concept. If others could do it so could I.

With music in my life, I began to smile, play and experience other words and worlds, other cultures and realized first hand that all white children were not on the A-track to success.

I soon joined the majority white Detroit All City Band. It was comprised of the best student players from the neighborhood schools and required a recommendation from the feeding schools' band leaders to audition. I became second chair, always fiercely competing with the Irish kid who was as determined to keep his first chair as I was to take it. This was the first time that I was exposed to the children of many cultures. The All City Band was a magnet for the city's best student musicians. The only advantage that most of the students had over me was that they had better and newer instruments; most took private lessons and didn't have to worry about eating at the end of the day.

Libraries

My introduction to libraries was at first a place
where I could hide. Libraries to street brothers
was kryptonite, an oxymoron to the tenth
power. Libraries in the Detroit of the 1950s
were white, quiet, safe and sacred places for
books, ideas and white children trying to feed
their minds and stay ahead. For me, the necessity
of libraries was early liberation to my young
mind and soul. I devoured their content like
running oil in the bad engine of a used car.
I was hot for knowledge and the more I received
the greater I realized the supreme ignorance of
my ways and that of my family.
For the first time, hope for me appeared on the
horizon with the acquisition of knowledge.
The finding of pure and practical answers that
seldom entered the Black community propelled
me into an aloneness that would never leave.

To talk about ideas—other than those of work,
eating, weekends, women and money placed me,
according to most brothers, on another planet. It
was like a musician discovering the beauty and
brilliance of Charlie Parker and Dizzy Gillespie,
realizing that their music was genius, and wondering if he could ever do that.
The real task was to get the young musicians to
try. Books and music encouraged me to try.

Maybe it was God, Damballah, or the supreme
judge who instructed my mother to ask me to go
to Detroit's public library to check out *Black Boy*
by Richard Wright. I, at first, refused to go
because I did not want to go to the white
library and ask a white librarian for a book with
Black in the title, authored by a Black
man who I was told was challenging white
America's concepts of itself and Black people.

Apartheid America had worked. I was completely ashamed of who I was, felt inferior, inadequate and unprepared to answer the simple question if asked "Why do you want to read *Black Boy*?"

I found *Black Boy* on the library shelf, there were two copies. I took one of them, walked to an un-peopled section of the reading room, sat down and began to read.

I was immediately captivated by the boldness of the language, the clarity of the ideas, the similarity of the writer's living experiences to my own, the familiarity of the landscape, the intellectual genius of the protagonist to get what he needed at any given time, the ability of Richard Wright to present a world in which our people were completely locked down emotionally, physically, economically and culturally, yet still functioned as whole human beings.

Each word, every sentence of paragraph after paragraph, page after page, was like a sledge-hammer hitting me up side my head, stating in no uncertain terms: Wake up Negro!

I checked out *Black Boy,* ran home, went to the room I shared with my sister and read all night. The next morning, upon completion of the book, the first serious book I read in less than twenty-four hours, I was not a different person but a different questioner. Wright gave me context for my own content.

I now had focus and direction for my own cultural and intellectual development. His works formed the circle for my own investigations into the ways and whys of white folks and my own life. Suddenly it slapped me right in the face, reading the right books, newspapers, magazines and journals and comprehending and questioning what one reads is fundamental to developing a critical consciousness and worldview. Knowledge of oneself, of one's culture is what shapes a person.

I do not know how my mother felt about the literature she read. We never talked about it. All I remember is that she wanted me to read. She was never angered by my spending countless hours in the library. As her life slowly slipped into another world, mine did too: into the pages of countless books that put me into other worlds, cultures, places and, without me knowing it, helped to determine my future.

Books and Music

Black music had freed me creatively, and Black literature was beginning to fine-tune me intellectually and culturally. For the first time in my young life, I realized that life had greater meaning than my present circumstances, and I began to chance a smile in-between books, concerts, and what I perceived as a fine girl's interest in me. I also picked up a pen and began to write my inner thoughts. I didn't call my words poetry, but they came like sweat in a twelve-round fight that you knew you couldn't win, but with proper training there was always a possibility of gaining ground, if only a yard, a word, or a round at a time.

There was, however, unending and enthusiastic talk about the music that was eating up the airwaves and nightspots for the young, Doo Wop.

55

Unlike much of the new jazz, Doo Wop was for dancing and getting close to the one you wanted. All of the basement rent parties, after school socials and church gatherings were venues for highlighting the newest Doo Wop recording and latest dances.

"The Glory of Love" by The Five Keys, "Crying in the Chapel" by the Orioles, "Money Honey" by Clyde McPhatter and The Drifters, "Goodnite Sweetheart, Goodnite" by The Spaniels, "Sh-Boom" by the Chords, "Gloria" by The Cadillacs, "Only You (and you Alone)" and "The Great Pretender" by The Platters and one of my favorites "Earth Angel (Will You Be Mine)" by The Penguins was the music that most young people of my generation lived for.

It was from 1955 to 1959 that I too became consumed by the music the churches could not hold back. The Cadillacs' "Speedo" and Frankie Lymon and The Teenagers' mega hit "Why Do

Fools Fall in Love" were some of the first crossover recordings that made these groups into national stars. There were many other hits such as "In the Still of the Night" by The Five Satins and "Oh What a Night" by the Chicago group, The Dells.' The Heartbeats came along with "A Thousand Miles Away" and The Dell Vikings came with "Come Go With Me" and "Whispering Bells." Soon, Jerry Butler and The Impressions impressed us all with their magnificent "For Your Precious Love." There were hits like "Shimmy, Shimmy, Ko-Ko-Bop"by Little Anthony and The Imperials; "Blue Moon" by The Marcels; "Daddy's Home" by Shep and The Limelites, as well as, any recording by The Drifters.

In 1959, the world of music forever changed and the Motor City of Detroit became Hitsville, USA with the introduction of Berry Gordy's Motown.

Used Books:
Finding Things of Value

I don't remember exactly when I discovered the importance of used bookstores. I do remember secondhand stores and Salvation Army outlets were instrumental to the way I dressed. Used, but clean, shirts and khakis acquired from Chinese laundries; coats, ties, suits, belts and shoes from the many church clothing sales defined my wardrobe. The Salvation Army store is where we furnished our apartments. I naturally gravitated toward the many used bookshelves that offered books by major writers for pennies.

I bought first editions of the works of Frank Yerby, Richard Wright and Ernest Hemingway for 15, 25 and 50 cents respectively in the 1950s. My personal buying habits developed early: books, music, weekly movies and occasionally spending on girls who didn't think me too odd or skinny.

My oddness can be attributed to my aloneness. It seems that my sister always had a social life. I, at a very young age, had taken on the difficult task of watching our home. Like most boys, I liked girls and many of them occasionally looked at me with more than negative comments about my clothes, quietness, bookishness or bonelike physique.

All the money I made went toward our keeping a roof over our heads and often to help buy food for dinner each day. I ate no breakfast, and I received a "free" lunch at school after I cleaned the cafeteria after the students finished eating their lunches. However, it was my reading, far above grade level, and the type of books that I consumed like water, that elicited the many questions about my life and that of Black people. Few girls that I wanted to date at fourteen wanted to talk about race.

The Neighborhood

I, like most boys in my community,
worked hard at whatever was available.
We collected junk from middle class alleys,
shined shoes outside train and bus stations,
worked in factories that made brooms and
mops, set pins in bowling alleys, helped my
mother clean white folks' homes in her last
days. I had a morning and afternoon paper
route. I bagged groceries, dropped policy for
the numbers trade, escorted women of the
night to their out-of-the-community callers,
cleaned up bars and taverns and became
a runner for the Black men who ran off-the-
book money trade. Hustling was not a calling,
it was a means to survival in a white world that
only allowed Blacks the droppings and back
stairs of economic survival.

Holidays

Holidays were the most difficult minutes of my
young life. Approaching Thanksgiving,
Christmas and Easter meant once again facing
our poverty, aloneness and disconnectedness.
Holidays are for families,
for bonding and renewed music,
for sharing strength, magic and love,
for bunches of smiles and yeses,
for innocent lovers and elder confirmations,
for giving, receiving and Christian commit-
ments, for children.

One Christmas stands out in my memory.
I was about thirteen and we lived in a wood
frame house next to the railroad tracks on the
east side of Detroit. The house was built with
cracks throughout its foundation. It literally
whistled in the winter and summer wind, and
we tried to fill the holes with cloth, mainly old
towels and when possible tacked the holes with

cardboard. In fact, cardboard fixed everything, especially the holes in my shoes. The only advantage living next to the railroad tracks was that often the freight trains that carried coal to the city's industries would park overnight outside our house, and I would steal coal from the open cars for our pot-belly wood and coal burning stove that set in the middle of our five room house. I would also walk the tracks, miles in each direction collecting coal that fell off the train as well as wood and other items that could be burned to warm our small house. It never was enough. We were always too cold in the winters or too hot in the summers. My nose never stopped running, no matter what the weather.

Christmas music played everywhere—in school, at church, in poor and high end department stores, on Black radio or what they called it at that time "race" radio. The Black or Negro musicians were beginning to cut Christmas songs and the best of the Do Wop groups recorded the season's standards such as "Silent Night." The soul that they put into that song made us believe that the birth of Christ was truly a virgin one. As a believer, "Silent Night" would often bring tears to my eyes because more than any other, it spoke to the essence of Christianity—the coming of a Savior.

In my younger years, Christmas music sparkled with hope, possibilities and engendered in me a feeling that if I were good, productive, honest and hard working that the holiness and goodness of the season would somehow, even in my wretched condition, touch me and my family. It never happened.

The Christmas I remember the most was the one we spent alone, without a tree, food or gifts. This was the one where my father promised us promises, and as usual he didn't fail to disappoint. I matured that Christmas and never cried again. When Easter arrived the following year, my father guaranteed me a new suit for church and the Easter "parade." This would be my first new suit.

Jimmy Lee arrived late with a light brown, almost orange outfit I accepted with no acknowledgement other than for him to witness me putting the suit in the garbage can as I exited out of the back door. By this time my very human expectations for a father's kindness in the form of love, food or gifts had died, along with my spirit.

Jackie: How Can I Protect You?

My sister at fourteen told me that she was
pregnant and as the man of the house, I went
looking for the man who was responsible. He
was the local gang leader, twenty-one years old
and full of himself. Upon seeing him, without
notice I hit him hard enough to get his attention. His retaliation, with the help of his men,
left me close to lifeless. I struggled home, clearly
physically and emotionally whipped and upon
seeing and questioning me my mother
"wooped" me again for getting "wooped."
During those times "good" girls didn't get
pregnant out of wedlock. My sister had been
overwhelmed and influenced by our condition.

We were the family that society missed. Our
poverty was not only economic but of the
spirit, soul and culture.

We lived off the books and never filed a yearly
income tax or worried about bill collectors who
could never find us. Each yearly move placed us
one apartment away from homelessness and
introduced us to the strangeness and strangers
of a new neighborhood, school, playmates and
will-less futures. The only permanent structure
in my young life was the Detroit Public Library
and the All City Band. Books and music were
the only hands of hope available to me.

My sister had her first child at fourteen, her
second at sixteen, third at eighteen. By the age
of twenty-seven, she had six children by four
different men.

Our grandfather said after she had her first
child, "she is hot now." I didn't understand
the comment at the time. He meant that the
sex pleasure principle had attached itself to her
very being. Little is said of the fathers of her
children. They disappeared into the bodies of
other women until they tired of playing the field
and decided that Jesus was truly calling them to
do right, which did not include supporting their
outside children.

Life Lesson: One

The lesson of the haves and have-less,
the cruelty of children, the unkindness of a
culture that creates teenagers who laugh at
those who don't have. It was at the Black mid-
dleclass of Plymouth Congregational Church
next door to our apartment building where the
cream of Black Detroit worshipped their God
each week. They arrived decked out in the
finery of the day, clean and cute and rushed.
Once I attended their young people's social in
my Chinese laundry shirt, Salvation Army sport
coat and tie, resale store shoes, pants and belt
and brand new Woolworth department store
socks. Clean. I walked into a freezer.

The girls, light and distant, brown and fine,
turned away with a smile and a nod. The boys,
suited and tied down in the selected threads of
their class, circled me issuing the cruelest of lessons, "you don't belong here."

I was crushed. Now, I had real life experiences with class divisions in the Black community. These "Negro" teenagers didn't even see me. I was not one of them and if I didn't know it, within 30 minutes of the social, I was standing alone with a cup of punch in my hand wondering, what in the hell was I doing here? I left frozen in shame and embarrassment. I told myself that these are not my people. They had become the "Black Bourgeoisie" of E. Franklin Frazier and the "Black Anglo Saxons" that Nathan Hare would eventually write about.

The Makings of a Poet

High school was music,
secret readings, work, study
and poetry writing.
No one saw my poems
or knew that I cared
after all, poetry was for girls.
Brothers catching me
head-deep into composing lines and rhymes,
noticing my pen to paper in non-paragraph form
wouldn't dare accuse me of poeting poetry,
then considered the weaker art.
I always responded with smiles and verbiage
"I'm writing lyrics for the Miracles and Four
Tops." Motown and Smokey Robinson often
saved my reputation as a real "man."

Aunt Sis

Aunt Sis, on my father's side was the closest relative who functioned without motive, other than love. Jesus was her savior and I was a favorite. Her smile was contagious and worked well with the white folks for whom she cleaned, ironed, washed and nannied. She left her pain on the job and never brought it home. She had the energy of twenty, and was always an easy hit for my father who always needed money.

She died at 93 and I never got to thank her in the manner deserving of her life of giving. Outside of my mother and sister, she was the closest and nicest relative on my father's side of the family. Her name was Penny Nicholson. She lived with her brother and his family. I don't believe that she ever married, and the Black church claimed her and never let go. The goodness of Jesus populated her speech and every time I would see her she had kind words about everybody as if she had never been hurt. She bathed in the warm sunlight of the Lord, and the Lord worked his magic on her soul and spirit.

The church had become her life and as an unofficial missionary, she intuitively worked the field of the uncommitted unbelievers, and it seemed to me that I was at the top of her list. I listened with deep respect, often without comment. She would always send me home with a dollar or two, a kiss on the forehead and the words I seldom heard from anyone, "I love you Dondi, be careful going home and trust in the Lord."

Helen Maxine

My mother was so beautiful that she not only stopped
cars, she stopped buses.
Her beauty, if just for a moment, made most men's
eyes roam and forget other women.
She was music unemployed.
She wrapped her body in clothes that refused to hide
the nature of her desires.
She wanted to be a dancer.
She wanted to be warm weather year round.
She wanted to know the origin of walnuts and wealth.
She wanted to play the harmonica
and sing like Billy Holiday. She believed in God, kind
Negroes, reciprocity and
southern food. Her clothes got in the way of men
taking them off.

Don: Man of the House

Boys become men too early
when fathers are not in the home.
I do not remember experiencing
a childhood. There was a brief year as a
boy scout. I played bugle in a Drum and
Bugle Corps. And learned chess at the
Boys Clubs of America, eventually becoming
the Club's Champion.

Everything else revolved around school and
work, work and school. I was making life-
determining decisions for myself,
my sister and mother too early.
I became the "man" of the house even
though "men" were always present.

Miss Barmaid of Detroit, 1948

My mother was Miss Barmaid of Detroit in
1948. She worked nights at Sonny Wilson's and
my sister and I were generally on our own.
Slowly, my mother was pulled into the fast life
of the streets. She was popular and dark-skinned
Black men enjoyed showing her off to their
friends. She was their prize for the night and the
missing period in our young sentences.

My mother had been forced into street culture
for survival, she was too beautiful to have
women friends, they all thought that she was
after their men. They thought their men had
nothing to do with it.

She broke many mirrors because her image was
not true. Her fear was ignorance, she did not
know how to solve the problem of her own

incompleteness and incompetence. She did not see a way out of not using her body for pleasure and finance. In using her body she was constantly reminded of her own "un-cleanliness" and she would wash and wash, bathe and bathe, until the only way she could adjust to the "un-cleanliness" was to drown herself into forgetfulness which arrived with the consumption of alcohol, drugs, sex and the feel good remarks of strangers.

Men of God

Many of the strangers were Black and white
ministers and a number of white God talkers in
white collars and Black suits.

Every church she attended the ministers would
make it their mission to introduce themselves
and hurriedly arrange private prayer and counsel
with her. I watched the men of God prostrate
themselves before her, most trying to own her
and when that failed they tried to shame her
with biblical language—that failed too.

Over a decade there were hundreds of ministers,
priests and significant numbers of rabbis who
never looked me in the eye. Men of God from
Detroit, Chicago, Indianapolis, Lansing, Ann
Arbor and environments in-between.

Helen Maxine: Two

Once I accidentally walked in on my mother and a customer having sex, she was covered by his body. I, at an early age, knew that she was working. I saw no enjoyment in her eyes, heard few cries of real pleasure or endearment.
In the room I shared with my sister, where I was always instructed to go when she was working, I consumed Black literature and dreamed of better days. I soon realized that sex was also an empowering tool for beautiful women who, like professional athletes, had less than a ten year window to make it or find another trade.

My mother, in her 34th year, four years on the other side of men lining up for favors and six years into the bottle and needle, ended up cleaning houses for white folks in-between the weekends of lost memory, sagging body and unending cries of a lost life. Seeing her like that tore my young heart apart, flawed my perception of the world and helped determine my decisions and lifestyle. I never drank alcoholic liquors, never been high, never smoked.

I viewed drunkenness as a weakness and a curse on our people. Without knowing it, at 14, I was searching for a healthy lifestyle and eventually I was to find it in the literature I consumed.

Janice

Janice, an acquaintance of my mother's, liked
men who liked danger. Her face was un-scarred.
It was her psychology that was battered. She
screamed about her boyfriend peeing on her to
help him come. Sick was not the word for most
of her relationships. She liked vanilla ice cream
with orange soda, a rather cheap dessert.
Actually it cost more than she ever received
from any of the fathers of her many children.

Janice lost her mother to the streets at the
tender age of seven. Her mother was too fine,
fancy, fast, fit-for-fun and famous. Men talked
about her like she was a professional sport.
She had a reputation for stealing men's hearts.
She called all her men farmers, stating with a
large smile that she was the earth that they

needed. The earth received Janice's mother at 29 years old. Janice was raised by an assortment of "stepfathers," aunts, friends, two foster homes and a man from the South claiming to be her mother's brother. She was on her own at twenty and had enough life experience to fill several police blotters. The men called her sweet. Janice was prettier than her mother and called her men, honey, so that she wouldn't have to remember their names.

The story is that Janice started going with one of her mother's boyfriends, a Mr. Keys. He was a bank vice-president at one of the local branch-es, also a respected family man with serious real estate and business holdings. Janice worked at one of his bars serving drinks and acting as all around hostess. She and her children lived in one of his houses. Janice thought that he loved her and that the house was actually hers. She had no papers and Mr. Keys told her repeatedly in the heat of getting some that the house was hers. Experienced women put statements like, "baby, I love you" and "you know I'll do anything for you" in the same category as "I'm going to leave my wife to marry you" or "you mean more to me than anything," as high fiction, as in say anything to get the pussy.

Mr. Keys was not a good man and his past was waiting to catch up with him. One Halloween night around 2 a.m. when Detroit was loud, awake and the bar was jumping, Mr. Keys and Janice were consuming a night cap. A man walked up to Mr. Keys and Janice, pulled out a nickel-plated 45, put it to Mr. Keys head, yelling out, "remember me, Nigger?" and pulled the trigger, blowing half of Mr. Key's head into Janice's lap, spoiling her tailor made suit. The shooter calmly walked out into the early morning night, never to be seen again. Janice saw her life slip away. Janice was not allowed to go to Mr. Key's last rites and a week after his burial she and her children were evicted from the house that she thought she owned. She told her children the truth, hoping that the truth would keep them from making her mistakes. For most of the children, teenagers then, such knowledge was too late.

Mable

Mable, a friend of Janice's, was winter. She had been made cold by years of maltreatment, rough by years of loneliness and false companionship and now in the middle of her time, refused to ever take another chance with a Black man.

Mable cursed the race. Didn't see no good that Black people had ever done. Raised on a plantation where her father was a sharecropper, she watched her mother, in her twilight years, steal away to Jesus. The Bible was more than solution, more than heaven after earth, it was food and water; it was ideas and values steeped in fear and peaceful salvation.

Mable ran North at twenty and between her twenty-first and twenty-seventh year visited every storefront church on the west and south sides of Chicago. She now fashions herself a true missionary of the living gospel. Her mission was to save Black men from their evil ways. She wanted Black men to be like Mr. Golding, the husband of the white woman where she did day work, for Mr. Golding took care of his family, had a big house and ate dinner with his family every night that he didn't have to work late (he worked late at least twice a week).

Most Black men thought Mable was fine but foolish. After loving, her, many would seek light fast. Disappear. Most leaving without an explanation. It came out later that some of them didn't like being preached at, at the point of sexual climax. Others felt that she prayed too much and were uncomfortable with being compared to Judas. After as many men as churches Mable, in her thirty-fifth year, decided to close her legs and like her mother give her life completely, to the only man in her life she declared had never failed her. Jesus would now be the only man in her heart. It is not known exactly when during that year she was called but rumor has it that the ultimate light touched her the day after Billy Williams, her last lover, started seeing her best and only friend Minnie Lou Turner.

Mable cursed the race. Didn't see no good in Black people. She turned slavishly and slowly toward her employers and began to live in Arlington Heights, Illinois, it was clean, peaceful and few black people lived there.

It was winter and windy, it was cold and white, and Jesus, sweet, sweet Jesus was her man.

The Catholic Church in our Neighborhood

The largest sanctuaries in our communities of the 1950s were Catholic churches. Not only were their buildings imposing, the children who went to their schools seemed to be orderly, well mannered and in a learning mode. They wore uniforms to school, the boys bright blue or white shirts with black ties and the girls white tops with plaid skirts. The one Catholic church in our neighborhood had one Black priest and two Black nuns, at least I think they were Black.

However, for me there seemed to be order, wealth and most of all peace. I started taking catechism at two Catholic churches looking for a way out of my misery. The teachers were young, white priests who knew nothing about Black people or Black culture. They were kind but foreign and remote. The twice-weekly lessons about the history, philosophy and belief system of the church left me somewhat cold, but I attended "faithfully" for about ten weeks until my many questions began to irritate the priests. The one question to which I never received a satisfactory answer: "Why do we call the priest, who is unmarried and supposedly celibate, father?"

Friends

Childhood friends were rare, only three come to mind: John McGee (White), Walter Sanford (Black), and Donald Berry (Black). John and I explored the neighborhood together unaware of color, culture, class or courage. As preteens, like most boys, we were learning to navigate the world and folks in tough places.

Walter and I spent countless hours learning the streets of Detroit and exploring the uncertainties of life between middle school and high school. He was my first and only Black friend in Detroit. Donald arrived in Dunbar Vocational High School in Chicago where girls occupied every living thought, especially the size of their breasts and the shape of their legs and butts. We studied in-between chasing girls and parted upon graduation. I understand he is still chasing girls. I took to chasing ideas and the politics and culture of Black liberation.

The First Time

I was rushed into sex by a professional.
I was 13, she was in her early twenties.
She worked with my mother and swore me to
secrecy. She said she liked me and wanted to
give me a gift.
Her magic started with a kiss, her tongue
touched the back of my throat.
She then moved to my dick that had already
enlarged, her lips upon my penis forced an
eruption almost instantly into her mouth.
She moved back to my mouth as
my member rose again as she climbed on me
and began to shake the earth. This was the first
of many, many, lessons.
I now understood why she and my mother were
in such high demand from the clergy,
politicians, and recent arrivals from the South.

I became her escort, sometimes 3 or 4 different
men a night. In the third year, on a 110 degree
night, she didn't return. They found her body
the next morning with a knife in her chest.
Her killer said he was in love, that she had to be
with him and no one else.

Women Talk

I learned early that
all Black men are not good lovers.
My mother and Janice would often
compare notes.
These conversations were not necessarily put
downs, but instructions on how
each woman fed the egos of scared men,
with small or large dicks who
did not know how to use them,
and worse didn't understand the art of sex or
the sexual psychology of women.
My mother and Janice shared secrets on
how to make Rev. so and so
feel like he was the only one,
the best lover ever and
assured him that if he wasn't married
that she would be on her knees everyday
serving him and only him.
Such sexual knowledge worked and for about

ten years my mother and Janice were able
to feed, house, clothe and educate their
children. They often stated that the egos of
most men are between their legs,
and bragging about their strength as lovers was
a universal rite of passage.

1955

Killers arrived early for
Black boys and men who did not
know or appreciate their place
in Money, Mississippi.
Emmett Till, a Chicago boy not much
older than me, joined the earth and our
ancestors on August 28, 1955 as a result of one
of the most brutal lynching ever recorded.
It was rumored that Emmett "whistled and
incorrectly" looked at a white woman. Her men
folk stole, in the heat of the Mississippi night,
Emmett's young life.

This was not just a killing, it was a ritual, a
lesson for Black boys and men. This was a
repositioning of boundaries, the putting of
hands on a boy by men who came in numbers;
as Sterling A. Brown writes, "not by ones, not
by twos, but by tens." These men, boosted by
their numbers and racial righteousness,
took a radiant possibility—Emmett—in the
night and the body returned to Chicago
unrecognizable. It was not just the bullet in the
face or the hatchet splitting his head, separating
eyeball from eyeball, or the forced ejection of
thirty teeth from his mouth, leaving only his
two front teeth partially holding his tongue
hanging loosely from his face like a child
screaming for mercy before the final drowning
and death blow. This was a "nigger stay in your
place" statement from a people, of a state,

in a nation, that has never respected or acknowledged Black people as human and sacred souls.

Emmett Till's body returned to Chicago locked down in a wooden box with orders not to be opened. A grieving mother, whose heart had already been chopped into pieces and snatched from her body comforted all who dared raise opposition to her seeing her son. Upon viewing his tortured, battered, blotted, mutilated, hacked and disfigured body, she realized that this crime of crimes ceased to be personal, ceased to be just about her baby. This was a national killing and the nation should, as quickly as possible, witness the cowardly work of their Christian sons.

Emmett Till's mother, Mamie, decided that her child's murder was not to be hidden in a closed casket with insufficient cries of racism and horror combined with pious sermons on evil and evildoers. This mother demanded that the world see what the nation did to her child. To the credit of John H. Johnson, publisher of *Jet Magazine*, the photographs of young Emmett's face appeared in the September 15, 1955 issue. People lined up at newsstands around the country to buy *Jet* and from that day on there was a new message in the nation. I heard the roar of Black people as I sold my thirty issues of *Jet*. I quickly went to the brother that distributed them in Detroit for more, but for the first time in his memory all over the nation the magazine sold out in less than 48 hours. Emmett Till's execution had touched Black hearts.

Africans born in America now saw the
end-game. White supremacy, nationalism, rage,
violence and ignorance sent us its message from
the hell-hole of Mississippi. Now, apartheid
America was public news, was state news,
was national news,
was world news,
because *Jet Magazine*, for that week
went against convention.
The Black community nationwide
put on muscle, shoes and resistance.
Earth shaking was beginning,
Emmett Till's murder helped
to flame a movement and march for freedom.
Mamie Till took up the memory of her son—
she did not let his death become history's
forgotten page.

In Alabama, a woman named Rosa Parks
was quietly readying herself
to give backbone to a nation of feet.
her act of defiance hurried our introduction
to a new Moses,
Martin Luther King, Jr.
The United States was soon to meet his,
ours and its history,
its future,
about to be rewritten.

Helen Maxine: Three

The beginning of my mother's end was when she could not start her day without a drink. Quickly that drink was followed by another and another until her body shut down.

I would seek out her hiding places for alcohol and drugs and destroy them. She would leave the house on Fridays and often didn't return until Sunday night or Monday morning. Often, I would search the local hotels and homes with rooms to let, seeking her out. I remember my many fights with strange men who had paid for a night or weekend and cared little about a son trying to protect his mother.

I, at 6'1", 131 pounds, did not inject too much fear in the hearts of men much larger than me. This was my advantage: I carried a lead pipe in my belt and could use it and the language of

the streets with a righteous certainty that
would force most men to stand down before
confrontation.

I was ready and willing to fight for Helen
Maxine Graves Lee—I was all she had.
And that was clearly not enough.

The Only Love That I Knew

The only love that I knew
was that of mother to her children
and son to mother.
I was losing my mother to forces
beyond my comprehension.
Her gradual decline
gained speed toward her end.
It was as if her voice slowed down
and her inability to function normally
advanced with each taste of alcohol.
Anger filled her body
like too many commas in a short paragraph.
Jackie and I could do no right in the eyes of her
many personalities. It was like seeing her
descend into a basement each night and
emerge the next morning with a new name,
we were on suicide watch.
She had lost her will to love us.

Music and Art

Music and literature taught me of love outside
of my immediate family. My mother and sister
had contained my young life. The musical
poetry of Miles Davis, phrasing and the
sentence and word music of Chester Himes and
Richard Wright short stories brought new
possibilities into my life. To play the trumpet
required serious discipline, required a way of life
that was new to me. I learned to breathe, read
and play music via the method of deep, critical
listening, practice, more practice and weekly
lessons. I learned to read, critically read,
literature and later write through the discipline
of study, thinking and single-minded concentra-
tion. Music and literature taught me the importance of discipline and self regulation and order,
taught me how to sleep and rise early with a
purpose greater than physical labor and missing
money. Inferior schools did not stop me. Music

and literature enlarged my universe of people and cultures. My skies ceased to be empty in the discovery of the many languages and landscapes of music, poetry and prose. Within their disciplines I discovered art and it was within the study of art I realized that life had meaning beyond watching my mother slowly die, my sister self-destruct, and the boys my age disappear into dead end streets, prisons and early graves. The study of art not only saved my young life, it gave me a life.

Seeking art forced me out of my community. I began to keep a journal where I would record my unusual interventions and conversations with strangers. As a poor boy, I was constantly searching for ways to earn extra money that would allow me to buy books and music (records and sheet music). I had become rather proficient as a young musician. I could read music as well as I read books. Put a new sheet of music before me, and one or two efforts at interpreting it was all I needed. I viewed music as a way out of the poor schools and restrictive neighborhoods that greatly limited my growth, development and desires. Cass Technical High School was the top high school in Detroit and clearly the one I wanted to attend. Students with a B+ or higher grade point average were allowed to test for entrance into Cass. I passed. Music and Junior ROTC were my passport into other cultures.

At Cass, I met other young musicians and we quickly formed a band with the hope that we could become good enough to perform at many

parties and non-school activities that required
live music. We all wanted to be like Miles,
Dizzy, Bird, Monk or any number of Black jazz
musicians who were changing the entire
landscape and conversation of progressive Black
music. We all tried to dress, walk, talk and play
like the Black musicians who had revolutionized
jazz. We were a sextet—the other five were
Black middle class boys and had none of
the family responsibilities that consumed much
of my time. They all came from intact families
and lived in homes where they had their own
bedrooms.

On the few occasions that I visited their homes
for band practice, I couldn't believe that Black
people lived so well. Out of the other five
members, three had parents who were teachers,
the other two were a doctor and a lawyer.

They all lived in homes with well attended front lawns and large back yards. Each of the children had their own bedroom and we practiced in what seemed to be a recreation room where their family relaxed and shared time together. They had functioning and proactive families where the children were made to feel secure, loved, wanted; each child was showered in a culture of growth and development.

In the home of the lawyer, the walls were carefully appointed with African and African American art. Both parents received me and the other band members as if we were a part of their extended family. The father, who loved jazz, showed us his extensive record collection and played the early records of Louis Armstrong for us. He also had a large library in his home, which was a revelation to me because I only conceived of libraries as being free-standing institutions or in public and private schools and universities. It was obvious that he was a well educated man and his wife, who was a pharmacist, was not an ignorant bystander. She played the flute and was the source of her son's love for music. She also spoke French and Spanish fluently and shared with us music from those cultures. I was impressed and forever influenced by all of their families. Each evening on the way home from practice I wished for what they had, knowing in the back of my reality it was not to be. At least I could dream.

Facing our History was like Vinegar on Open Wounds

There was little peace in our apartment. The smallest of disagreements was reason for verbal or physical battles. I recall a serious fight over nothing where I had to pull our "stepfather" off my mother with a butcher knife and threaten him with death and after death, if he ever laid a hand on her again. I was 16 approaching 36 and my emotions had long ceased to engender smiles in my soul. I had become stone as my mother's condition worsened each day. The lowest season of my remembrance was when she stole my bank and used my savings to feed her habit. This act of stealing from her son confirmed in me the absolute danger and the forbidding culture of drugs.

This lesson governed my life. I have never drank, never tried drugs; I am probably one of the few Black men in the world who grew up in a culture steeped in alcohol and drugs, spent close to three years in the military and have never been intoxicated.

Helen Maxine Graves Lee, mother

The Graves children,
Helen, (center) Mayme and Johnny

Johnny Graves, uncle

Don L. Lee/Haki Madhubuti: Fort Bliss, Texas

Fort Bliss, Texas

Dunbar High School,
Chicago. Age 18

Walter Sanford,
High School friend

Jimmy Lee, Haki's father with
second wife, Juanita

Donald Berry,
High School friend

Jacklyn Lee, sister

Haki adopted Paul Robeson and W.E.B. Dubois
as his cultural grandfathers.

Helen Maxine:
The Last Conversation

The last conversation my mother and I had was
a fight. I had bought two new shirts to wear for
special occasions at school. I was an A student
and frequently called upon to represent my class
or the school in academic or musical contests
and presentations. The morning of a major
event I could not find one of my shirts.
My mother had worn it the night before
and was fast asleep in it.
I couldn't control my anger and
brought her to tears with my hurt and utter
dissatisfaction of my life, her life,
my sister's life and our general existence.
Within a week she was dead.

Making Transitions

My mother never recovered from the many
noises in her life. What I remember of her
going-home ritual is that complete strangers
said nice things about her and the casket was
not open. I wore my first brand new suit
without a tie, sitting in the front row with
family members I did not know. I could not cry.
My sister, with a new baby in her arms, did not
dry her eyes that week. I was on my own. My
sister and her baby were on their own and we
didn't have a security or escape net. She went
to my grandfather's church and home for help.
I didn't. A family member asked why I stopped
going to church. I said that it "affected my
relationship with God." That next week I was
on a Greyhound bus to Chicago. I was
seventeen, on my own, going to seek help
from a stranger—my father.

For Helen Maxine Graves Lee

Helen Maxine Graves Lee was here.
Her son knew it, her daughter loved it.
There wasn't a terrible artery to her heart
her blood flow was warm and ancient
accenting her human kindness and mercy
which translated among the urban walkers
as weakness, naiveté and fragile weather.

She loved God.
She loved the men of God.
Through him and them she searched
and reached for salvation.
They populated her bed and head,
pleasured themselves, moved in and out of
her life like a Los Angeles rush hour
in the heat of hot sex.
She lost her God.
The men of God only noticed
her weight gain and less frequent smiles

113

as she accepted their pennies and criticism
without comment or eye contact.

Her's was a pure heart,
her son knew it,
her daughter learned it,
the men of God continued on their way
finding newer and younger
Helen Maxine Graves Lees.

Jimmy Lee:
A Lesson from my Father

My father received me

with the pleasure of a bad toothache,

and/or an ugly woman.

There was no music between us.

I feared him.

I do not know what he thought of me.

There was never any conversation between us.

No hugs, no kisses, no congratulations

on good grades, no encouragement,

no question about my feelings or

that of my sister's well being.

Just brutal criticism.

Our time together was short, hostile

and without any redeeming qualities.

The one lesson I learned from him was

how not to be a father.

I never saw my father with a book in his hands.
Yes, he could read and had a mind that worked
faster than children consuming Sunday morning
pancakes and maple syrup. He could talk his
way into a woman's body or out of harm's way
without coming up for air. He lied like most
people tell the truth, with complete conviction.
He lived on his own timetable and intuition,
always under the radar screen of "legal" white
commerce.

Jimmy Lee knew the streets and the streets
knew him. He was always clean, drove a late
model car, kept money wrapped tightly in a
rubber band in his left pants pocket. He
refused to answer questions from most people;
his business was his business. He was a lot
"freer" than most of us because he understood,
even though he never articulated it to me—that
we, in America were un-free. He was a man of

large ideas living in a world that did not, and
would not respect or recognize the exceptionality
and genius of Black people. That he survived, in
the context of his people's survival, always living a
few levels above those he made his living off is a
profound comment on his knowledge of, and use
of the limited economics of Black belt communities.

His life was always quick money. The weekends,
after Black workers received their weekly pay was
when Jimmy Lee and his kind went to work. He
knew the weaknesses of an enslaved people looking
for a little, just a little fun and joy for their over-
worked and under appreciated lives. Whether it was
the numbers game, night life, drugs or alcohol,
women or cards, or any kind of gambling he had
his hands in it most of his life. And, as far as I
know, he never spent a night in jail.

Jimmy Lee and Don

There was no love lost between Jimmy Lee and
me because none ever existed. I understood
him. He worked the outside express lanes and
chose to never come into side streets. One had
to have a special key to unlock his emotions.
His attitude towards me became negative re-
enforcement. I took his sense of independence,
love of music and women, his artistic leanings
and attempt to make a life, the exact opposite of
an outlaw. It was not that I didn't break the
"rules" of conventional society, I did, I just
didn't allow the laws of the street to become a
part of my interior as the only "way."

In my many moments of questions, I turned to
books. Reading was like consuming food, an
absolute necessity if I were to live anywhere on
the edges of normality. It was in Black literature
where I received my ultimate lessons of life. It
was white Western literature that gave me a

head-start in finding my place as a poet/writer/
activist. The insights that I found as a young
man can be attributed to the hundreds of books
that I read between the ages of thirteen and
twenty-one. And, rather than staying up late at
night talking to myself or to the wall, I started
talking to the blank page. I began to write. My
father, in his own way, was partially responsible
for my becoming a poet and community activist.
His independence, his Black boldness, his ability
to take little or nothing and make a wave or a
bridge to profit or under a fine woman's skirt is
what kept him alive and, in his mind, free. I
only viewed this from the outside; he never let
me into his interior. Did it hurt? I doubt it.
Did it affect me? Yes, in ways that I am still
discovering. Surely my ability to run toward
fear has been a part of my operating instructions
from day one.

Fathers and Priests

I was to meet raw evil often and fight it.
It was the pure evil that I was not prepared for.
I could see potholes in the hearts of men,
understood the racial tracking of my education,
studied the economic inequalities of waged
labor, the exclusivity of certain neighborhoods
and the absolute privilege of white skin color.
I realized early the psychological advantage of
priests demanding parishioners call them father
as they unzipped the pants of young boys. My
street-wise question to one of them: "Father,
why must I take my pants off to pray?" After I
laid him out with my lead pipe, I left the church
and never returned.

1960

I graduated from Chicago's Dunbar High School in 1960, completing a two-year curriculum in one year and a summer. I attempted to join the United States Air Force but was rejected because of a heart murmur. Solicited by a *Chicago Defender* ad, I joined a Black magazine selling group. Two cars of teenagers with two adults traveled South, stopping in Black communities to hawk magazine subscriptions. My sales pitch and lie was that I was working my way through Howard University.
I knew about Howard from reading Sterling A. Brown, Rayford Logan, Alain Locke and E. Franklin Frazier. I inherited my father's skill at selling. I could sell dirt to a housewife and dried shit to a junkie.

Door to Door: The Art of Language

I learned how to lie, rap, steal, fight and survive most urban landscapes on the streets of Detroit and Chicago. Approaching the homes of Blacks in the southern cities of Illinois to sell magazine subscriptions was a breeze. I used the language of my self-education in defining the absolute necessity of *Ebony* and *Jet* to understand the internal workings of the national Black community. I was the top salesman; as most new subscribers paid for their magazines they wished me well at Howard University. In Springfield, Illinois, the capital, I met many Black professionals who worked for the state. In my dark blue suit, the one I got for my mother's funeral, white shirt and dark tie, I started my day at a home that looked promising. An elderly Black man answered the door and I immediately went into my sales pitch of working my way through Howard University. To my amazement he was a

Howard University Law School graduate and
welcomed me into his home. I knew I was in
trouble.

In an excited state this dignified looking Black
man questioned me about my studies at
Howard University and life in the city of
Washington, D.C. Almost instantly he realized
that I was lying about my Howard experience.
Rather than jump into my chest and throw me
out, he asked if I was hungry. While his wife
fixed me a sandwich, he bought a subscription
to *Ebony, Jet* and *Life*. As I ate the sandwich, he
quietly exposed me and stated in a fatherly
manner that one of the few acts that truly
advance Black people is a quality education and
that knowledge and academic credentials are
indispensable in a racist, industrial and

knowledge-based society. He said that one's education could never be taken away. I explained to him that I was alone and had few other options, which was why I was selling magazine subscriptions. He told me about the new two year community college programs that were coming to most states and that they were developed for people with few resources. He had a smile in his eyes and frequently called me son. This was the first time that anyone had called me son, and coming from this accomplished Black man, it got my total attention. I relaxed and smiled back with tears in my eyes. This was the first time that *any Black man* spent quality time with me, expecting nothing in return, and the first time I let a stranger see my heartfelt emotions. My emotions exploded because he called me out of my name in a way that exhibited love and caring. He called me *son*.

As I got up to leave, I thanked him profusely
for his food, the subscriptions, his advice and
for his unexpected hospitality. As I opened the
door, he called me to wait. He went into his
wallet and pulled out a twenty dollar bill, folded
it into a quarter-fold and told me to put it into
my wallet for an emergency. I couldn't believe
his act of generosity and kindness. It actually
brought greater tears to my eyes. Twenty dollars
in 1960 is close to 100 dollars in today's money.
The thirty minutes I spent with this Black elder
helped to shape my young life.

I became ill in East St. Louis. The group with
whom I was traveling left me in the Booker T.
Washington Hotel. When I recovered, I used
the twenty dollars to pay the hotel bill. I went
into St. Louis, found the poor man's bank-pawn
shop, and pawned my trumpet (Miles Davis
playing encouraged me to pick the trumpet up

and Louis Armstrong, in all of his magnificence made it clear to me I could never play that well, so I put it down), slide rule and suit, and joined the U.S. Army.

During my physical, I went to the youngest looking doctor in the room. He inquired about my heart. I told him that I was nervous and that I had never been around this many white people in my life. I passed the physical and had no idea of what awaited me other than I would be able to eat regularly, get paid, and have a bed to myself. Oh, and new clothes: the uniforms of the United States Army.

——Part Two——
The Making of Men

Basic Training

At six o'clock on a cold October morning, we arrived at Fort Leonard Wood, Missouri for basic training. Four buses of men, all white except two other Black men and me. I was reading *Here I Stand* by Paul Robeson and had it in my hand as I stepped off the bus. The drill sergeant, a slim hard white man in his late thirties, upon noticing Paul Robeson's big Black determined face on the cover, snatched the book from my hand and barked into my face, "what's your Negro mind doing reading this Black communist?" Jumping with fear, I thought it was the first time I heard a double negative used so creatively. This was October of 1960 and Paul Robeson, W.E.B. DuBois and Langston Hughes, among others, had been abused by the House Sub-Committee on Un-American Activities. He continued, "all you women up against the bus." Of course, no women were among us; this clearly was the start of Army re-education. With my book high above his head, he commenced to tear out the pages and gave one to each recruit, demanding it be used for toilet paper.

This was a loud awakening to the military. I stood there cold, afraid, and alone that October morning. I and two other Black men were in a sea of whiteness in the wilderness of a foreign culture. I could only recall the instructions from John O. Killens lecturing on his yet-to-be released novel about Black men and World War II, *And Then We Heard The Thunder*—"when outnumbered, keep your mouth shut and think of your options, if any."

The destruction of my book encouraged me to find another copy as quickly as possible.

I was Black and in the U.S. Army rather than
the U.S. prison system. I had learned to never
apologize for being Black and to arm myself
with facts about the strength of my own
culture. Also, in the middle of military culture,
learn it, be effective in it, but be more apprecia-
tive and effective in your own culture. Go on
the offense, be the best, anticipate and respond
forcefully while understanding the importance
of ideas and their consequences. Ideas and the
creators of new ideas run the world.
Where are the African ideas?
Where are the Black ideas?
Who am I? What is your real name?
I arranged to have half my monthly pay sent to
my sister and went about the serious business of
learning my real name and being a soldier.

A Test of Leadership

Because of my short introduction to Army life
in the JROTC at Cass Technical High School,
I was able to adjust to Army life rather easily.
In basic training, I was appointed a squad
leader. All the men in my squad were white, all
were older than me and clearly not happy with
me as their immediate leader in the chain of
command.

The military layered my life, forced to dry
shave, do one-arm pushups in my sleep, master
the mechanics of weapons and in-step marching.
I took to warrior-hood like a pig to corn.
In uniform, I was a natural order-taker and
giver. I only woke up when I was required to
think about why I ceased to think. Basic training was easier and safer than walking the streets
of Detroit or Chicago. I learned to strategically
fight by avoiding fights, but when confrontation

called, retreat was not a part of the blood-game.
I was denied Officer's Candidate School because
I asked and answered too many questions and
didn't smile enough at the right time. I would
have been a good officer, I liked discipline and
structure. If I had the chance, I would have
been the perfect candidate for West Point, but
as my father would often say, "it ain't in the
cards." I ate three meals a day for the first time
in my life. I lost my 6'1" thin as a rail frame and
bloomed into a 6'1", one hundred and sixty
pounds of hard flesh and bone.

I Waited

In 1960 the U.S. Army's motto was "hurry up
and wait." I waited with books, I waited with
ideas and uncertainties,
I waited with my writing journals,
I waited with the poetry of Langston Hughes,
Carl Sandburg, Paul Laurence Dunbar, Claude
McKay, Melvin B. Tolson, Gwendolyn Brooks,
James Weldon Johnson, and Waring Cuney.
I consumed the works of Sterling A. Brown,
Margaret Walker, Robert Hayden, Countee
Cullen and Frank Marshall Davis.
I waited with the non-fiction of W.E.B. DuBois,
Monroe Trotter, Ida B. Wells,
Carter G. Woodson, E. Franklin Frazier,
Rayford W. Logan, and Melville J. Herskovits.
I waited with the fiction of Richard Wright,
Zora Neale Hurston, Jean Toomer, William
Faulkner, Frank Yerby, Chester Himes and
Dorothy West.

I waited with the music of Detroit's Motown,
Chicago's blues and New York's progressive
jazz. I waited with the bright future stories of
Jet, Ebony, the *Michigan Chronicle, Chicago
Defender* and the "New Negroes" of Alain
Locke. For the two years and ten months of my
service, I read close to a book a day.
Literature and music were more important to
me than clothes, cars, weekend furloughs, and
chasing women.

Learning in the Wilderness

The largest fraternity in the United States
is the one of military men, women and families.
The culture of men training and fighting
together is older than the nation. As old as
thought and history. I'll never forget my
military training and the lessons learned.
The trials won and lost prepared me for danger.
I acquired the mindset needed for confrontations and winning at any cost, for understanding
the buddy system, wilderness and night training,
reading the eyes of enemies, learning wilderness
strategies, landscape navigation and the
mysteries of maps, while comprehending the
proper use of weapons and fighting at one's
advantage. My first reading of Sun Tzu's *The
Art of War* and Lao Tzu's *The Way of Life* live
with me today.

I adapted to sleep depravation and learned the use of everyday objects as deadly weapons. Above all I was taught to act in such a way to never, and I mean never, by one's brother or foe to ever be called one of the most sexist of terms, a pussy.

Fort Leonard Wood in October 1960 was called Little Korea and as far as I knew lived up to the designation. Its terrain issued pain indiscrimi-nately. Within three weeks, I was hard as stone and knew that I would not survive the eight weeks without serious confrontations with the men in my squad. I, in this culture of "men" had no one to turn to, to run to, to share my fear with, which forced me to learn how to go deeply inside to confront my own insecurities and just as important, I learned to prepare my mind, body, soul, and spirit to operate as one.

President Truman had signed an executive order to finally integrate the armed forces; however, it did little in changing the hearts and minds of new recruits who were more often than not poor, young, beginning racists, unmoving in their own white skin privilege and without a doubt knew that Christ was the Lord and that all others were unbelievers and were ripe and ready for the kill. John Wayne and his likes, as well as the text books of the rural and urban high schools, had prepared them well enough to take orders without questions, to honor the flag above one's own life, and if ordered would without question unleash hell on earth with the quickness of dropping a clip of ammo into an M-1 to fire at any human not white.

Two Opposing Armies

In the fourth week of basic training, two stories began to circulate around our company. The first was that there was a rich white boy from the East beating everybody in chess; and second, the best squad in the company was headed by a Negro and all he did in his spare time was read. The only time that I had been close to money, I mean real money, was upon meeting Winford G. Smith (not his real name). His father owned something big and his act of joining the U.S. Army was, as he explained it, a way of exerting his independence. The problem was that the Army doesn't allow for independence. Any liberated soul had to be contained: push-upped and kitchen-patrolled into his senses.

Winford was a pinkish skinned white-white man. You could tell right away that he was out of his element. He liked telling people what to do.

He also knew more than most of us having earned his undergraduate degree from Harvard at the age of nineteen. He was in Harvard's Law School when he and his father had a disagreement that pushed him into joining the military. This act was, ultimately not so much a show of independence or individuality, but done to hurt his father and family. However, whatever the problem was it ceased to exist within that third week of basic training, beginning the fourth Friday, a private plane would land close to the base to take him back east for the weekend.

Because of his education and due in part to my habit of reading each night, we often shared thoughts beyond the ordinary. He was not in my squad and, therefore, our relationship did not compromise my leadership. He defined

himself as an avid chess player and asked if I
knew the game. I lied and said, No, although I
became the local Boys Club champion in
Detroit in 1958. I let him think that he was
teaching me the game as I watched, played and
learned his game and strategy. In the following
days, he was beating all comers. The white
soldiers regularly played chess like it were
checkers and most could not, did not, conceive
of an entire game before the first move. As
Winford played three, four and five moves
ahead of most of his opponents they fell into his
traps and were easily relieved of a good portion
of their monthly pay. He had his class sense of
invincibility. Of course, Winford did not need
the money–depending on his opponent he
would keep it all and sometimes lose on purpose
in order to entice someone whom he didn't care
for into a game solely to take his money. He

did not come from a chess-playing family. As he tells it, he was a first generation chess player. His father was into golf and football. In fact, he stated rather proudly that he grew up in country clubs sprinkled along the East Coast.

I tired quickly of Winford's superior attitude and arrogance. What bothered me the most was that he truly represented his class. Before the fourth week of basic, he was paying other men to shine his boots, make his bed, do his KP and guard duty, run errands for him, and anything else that his money would allow him to get away with. It was clear that the company commander, and other commissioned officers had been bought off because Winford started leaving on Thursday evenings for long weekends. Many of the NCOs also enjoyed his bounty; Winford began to spend too much time

not training with the rest of the company. I
approached the two other Black men in the
company and offered them an opportunity to
make some money. I made it clear to them that
I could easily beat Winford and that we should
pool our money behind my game. We came up
with $550.

I understood the game, and money always talks.
One evening after Winford had beaten everyone
who dared to challenge him, he took my bait.
The men gathered around to see the "Negro"
and the white-white man play. Winford in all
his arrogance began to use our game as a lesson
for those he had previously beaten. I purposely
let him beat me for the first two games, losing
about fifty dollars. And as taught by my father,
upon the third game, I bet a month's pay plus
the money I had borrowed from the two Black

men in the company, promising them a good return on their investment. I put $500 on the table.

Winford, fronting his education and privilege, doubled the bet, which I could not match. However, one of the white NCOs who had also tired of this rich white boy peeing on his parade, decided to back my game and put $500 of his money in the pot matching Winford's. I knew his game. I understood his limitations. I, too, had been schooled in the fine art of chess thinking. I not only played well but also studied the literature. But most importantly, Winford was at best a mediocre player. The problem was that he had no real competition in his company. I knew this, and I knew that I could beat him almost with my eyes closed.

As the game started, I could easily read his eyes
and body movements. He was too full of himself
and his cockiness and certainty, only highlighted
his elementary mistakes allowing me to check-
mate within twenty moves. The beautiful aspect
of chess is that it is almost impossible to cheat.
Most certainly, in our third game, without a
clock, it was just the two of us, the board, the
two opposing armies and a gathering of soldiers
witnessing a Black boy of exception boldly
beating a Harvard-educated white boy at his own
game and not breaking a sweat or a smile.
Of course, Winford was extremely upset and
quickly challenged me to another game. But I
had also learned from watching my father at
poker, it is not good to ever get too full of your-
self after winning, especially around people who
don't like you. I refused another game stating
that I was just lucky, it was late, and lights were

to be turned off in about fifteen minutes. And stating let's try this another day.

Another day did not come. Before the final week of basic training, Winford G. Smith's money got him out of the Army, never to be heard of again.

I shared a bunk with an overweight farm boy from Iowa. I on the top, he on the bottom. The other men of the company had little empathy for him or his weight. As his squad leader, I tried to help him, but his commitment to his kind, to his own cultural brothers, continued to interfere with our communication. My squad was the best in the company. We were the best marksmen, we ran the fastest, could do unlimited pushups, understood the fine points of hand to hand combat and excelled in close quarter marching. I pushed them and they hated me. The first seven weeks of basic training matured me, for young men it is indeed a life transforming experience, a rite-of-passage, not unlike, in many ways, a young woman giving birth for the first time. The mind and body are changed forever. The lessons learned could be stairs to climb upon if one is in a learning mode or if one is truly destined to be the back pages of everybody's history. It can all be wrapped up in one word-difficult. The non-commissioned officers ran us ragged; from sun-up to sun-down we seldom stopped for anything other than a quick breakfast, lunch and dinner. We had an hour or so each night to write letters, but beyond that, most certainly for the first four weeks, every breathing moment was spent on creating a new kind of person. The U.S. Army was in the business of producing men who would be the first line of defense, or as in some cases, offense for the nation. Men who could take and give orders regardless of rank and circumstances.

Partially due to my size, I never learned to fight as a teenager without the advantage of some kind of weapon: a lead pipe, a steel lock on my middle finger or a knife. In the Army I took up boxing but never became proficient enough to do any real harm to those who wanted to do me damage. However, I did learn to understand and appreciate the difficult sport or as some describe it the "art" of boxing. I grew up listening to the fights of Joe Louis and Sugar Ray Robinson. Joe Louis fought with the race of his people in his fist and the Sugar Man epitomized in the ring the dancer he wanted to be.

Most of the men I served with in basic training were older and had some time in the National Guard or Army Reserve. Many had finished college and had already started families and careers. Two nights before bivouac (the final week of field training), at about three o'clock in the morning, I was asleep.

Several of the men threw a blanket over me and pushed my bed to the floor. I, as accustomed, was sleeping with my trench shovel and upon hitting the floor came up ready to fight. They ran down the stairs out of the barracks. I caught one, hit him a couple of times, reported him to headquarters and he was recycled for another eight weeks. This act increased their dislike of me. I was told by one of my attackers that I had better not come on bivouac, that I might not make it back alive. I hit him and told him to tell his cowardly friends to bring it on. Of course, it was my youth, Chicago/Detroit toughness and Army macho talking and not me. I was scared shitless. I was alone and knew in the rhythms of their calmness they were serious.

The first three days of field training I slept very little. Luckily, much of our training was night work. The fourth night, I was completely out on my feet. I turned in early in the two-man tent that I shared with the man from Iowa. I do not know if he was aware of the threat. By 9 p.m., my bones were glued to my sleeping bag, and I was deep into dreaming about Army life and survival. About 2 a.m., the poles holding up each end of the tent were snatched out of the ground causing the tent to fall on us. Upon hearing the earth move as a result of their actions, I immediately, almost instinctively,

pulled the boy from Iowa on top of me. It was
he who caught the full impact of the shelves
breaking his spine. His screams woke the camp
as his brothers ran for cover. They broke his
back, and he was helicoptered out of the field to
the base hospital. I never heard from him after
that night.

I was segregated out for my own protection. We
graduated from basic training five days later. As
I received my certificate, I noticed the families
of all of the other newly minted soldiers with
girlfriends, wives, mothers, fathers and siblings.
I not only stood alone, I felt alone—a feeling
that would ride me life-long. I was rotated out
for advanced training at Fort Bliss in El Paso,
Texas. I was reading W.E.B. DuBois' *The Souls
of Black Folk*. Dr. DuBois' *The World and
Africa* was next on my list, and a racial

consciousness was ringing hard and fast in me, causing me to question everything, every action that white people claimed for the world. My life ceased to be circles and surfaces. My two years and ten months in the military were essentially my undergraduate education.

During basic training, I was taking the Evelyn Woods Speed Reading course. I was trying as hard as possible to read for substance and clarity, looking for the protein in each paragraph. I was already reading with a pen or pencil in my hand, and all of my books had questions and remarks in the margins of each page. I viewed each book as a conversation with the author. I began to read more non-fiction than fiction. Also, I read poetry each night before "lights out." It was clear to me that each book empowered me intellectually. Often, I was questioned by other soldiers, many

wanting to know why I stayed in the post
library so much. I read close to a book a day,
concentrating in history, political science, Black
literature, and (of course) Black poetry—the
written/oral music of our people. As I read and
studied the history and culture of Black folks I,
without knowing it became empowered, and my
temperament emerged as short and hostile to
the ignorance of others, Black and white.

January, 1961—El Paso, Texas

Texas was new territory for me. I had never been
southwest of Missouri. El Paso was on the border
of Mexico and Juarez was the soldier's play-
ground. My "advanced" training was in missile
control and guidance. The only positive aspect of
this new posting was there were more brothers in
my company. Eight Black men, six from large
urban areas and two from the South.

One of the brothers from the South was an
amateur boxer, and he looked the part. Tall, dark
skin, big smile, with missing front teeth, replaced
with gold and possessed with the unique ability to
stare a hole in a skillet. He was walking danger
and talked very little. We quickly became friends.
I helped him with his writing and reading. He
schooled me in self-defense and advanced boxing.

In keeping with the national culture, the racial
conflicts that existed in Texas between Blacks and
whites were multiplied in the close quarters
in which we lived. The difference here was that I
was with a fellowship of Black men who had no
fear, even though white soldiers outnumbered us
at least ten to one. The big mistake the white
soldiers made, no doubt swimming merrily in
their own notions of white supremacy and
numbers, was to constantly challenge us as men.
We accepted their invitation to battle with a one-
on-one contest to settle our differences. Our
man, one-on-one against their man. We gladly
fixed the date, time and place. Of course, it had
to be after work hours and off base.

I thought that we trained hard in basic training.
Willie, our man, upon accepting the challenge to
fight for our side, immediately went into hyper-

training. Rising at 5 a.m., running four miles, and gym-training with large and small boxing bags, he used each of us as sparing partners, not that we gave him any serious competition. He felt he needed a body in front of him to hit at once in awhile, a great while. When we were allowed to hit his hard body it was probably more painful to us than him. He was faster than popping pop- corn, his foot speed was like that of an antelope escaping the teeth of a lion. However, it was his eyes that burned into us his desire to win. Willie saw everything. Before an opponent's punch was thrown, he had already countered. I noticed the coordination of his body, the quickness of his hands and feet, the way he leaned toward an opponent, throwing punches or moved away avoiding punches. All had to do with what he saw and his conditioning. He looked at an opponent's chest to measure his distance and the velocity of his attempts. He was, as best as I could tell, scientific about his preparation. He often talked about Sugar Ray Robinson as the model boxer. He said that Joe Louis was his hero, but the Sugar Man was his teacher.

The fight was scheduled for a Saturday afternoon in a boxing gym in the Mexican-American community of El Paso. We picked the place for the fight because we felt we needed to be in a neutral and "safe" part of town. The word got out and over two hundred men showed up, about 135 white men and the rest Black and Mexican.

Willie, upon seeing his opponent, all 6'5", 255 pounds of him smiled and said to me that this was going to be fun. Willie was 6'2", a hard 175 pounds and knew something we didn't.

What he saw upon viewing Larry, the white representative and "their great white hope" of that day was that he was not a fighter or boxer. Willie later told me that Larry, without a doubt could not hold his own in a bar room or barracks fight. He knew by the way he walked to the ring. The way he climbed through the ropes, the dryness of his skin before the fight and his uneasiness upon seeing him.

By contrast, Willie was sweating profusely, warmed up and dancing to the center of the ring for the referee's instructions. Willie, "gold tooth among his white," smiled at Larry, a non-menacing, almost apologetic smile as if he felt sorry for this giant of a white man. Upon returning to our corner Willie whispered to me, "you could beat this guy." With those comments, I knew that we had a winner and I told the brothers to double all bets. The whites, most of them sure of winning against this much smaller man easily walked into our trap. Their money on their man exceeded all expectations. The odds were three-to-one against our man. We quickly pooled our money looking forward to three times our investment.

During the first round Willie and Larry used their jabs and danced around each other, both waiting for the other to make a move. They used the round to feel each other out and few power punches were thrown. In round two Larry picked up the pace and Willie, keeping within the game plan, allowed Larry to hit him without damaging retaliation. In fact, we could all see the confidence in Larry grow all out of proportion as he landed his jabs and overhand rights.

On one occasion Willie allowed Larry to back him into a corner and without too much effort ducked and danced his way into the offensive position with blows to Larry's midsection. Larry walked through what he felt was all the power Willie could muster and caught Willie with a right uppercut which caused Willie to smile and back away as the bell rang, ending round two.

I learned another valuable life lesson that day. After Willie carried Larry for two rounds all the bets had been placed with the odds against us—in some cases now five to one. Willie was given the go—ahead and in the third round, knocked Larry down twice and knocked him out before the end of the round. The white soldiers, without exception, had placed the status of their high station in life in our company on the ability of

their man to beat our man. But not just to beat
him, but beat him badly. Their confidence grew
out of proportion when their man, who had at
least thirty pounds on ours, stood toe-to-toe
with Willie with a menacing smile on his face. It
was clear to me that the size of the competitor
or foe is not necessarily the greatest problem. It
is how one uses what he has and one's ability to
maximize one's talents and develop winning
skills and minds that will determine the out-
come.

After Willie knocked Larry out, he went to the
center of the ring to help him back to his corner
and did something that none of us expected.
He thanked Larry for a good fight and told
him to keep up the good work. This show of
sportsmanship and good manners in winning
tempered how all of us responded to the win.

We quietly collected our money, walked Willie to
the locker room and waited while he showered
and dressed. We waited until all of the white
soldiers left and then we, along with the Mexican
G.I.s, celebrated. From that day forward, we
had no more difficulty with the whites of our
company or any company on that base. The word
had spread like wild fire on gasoline Newsprint—
leave the Blacks alone.

Last trip to Juarez

Army life and thinking are natural antagonists.
My reading forced me to question almost every-
thing. I had completed DuBois' *The World and
Africa* and was reading Carter G. Woodson's
The Mis-education of the Negro, a work that was
clear, current and spoke directly to my condition.

DuBois and Woodson challenged me to question
all things political, social and economic in reference to the Black-White situation. The officers
and NCOs tired quickly of my inquisitions, and I
suffered dearly because of a perceived arrogance.
The military is a top down command structure
and to succeed, one must be able to follow
orders no matter how ridiculous. There was a
manual for everything written at an eighth grade
level.

Just before graduation, I joined the brothers on their last trip into Juarez, Mexico. They would go just about every weekend to "buy sex" from Mexican women. I used all of my free time to study. After Willie's celebratory win, I decided to go. I grew up in the sex trade, and this trip did not excite me. I went because Willie asked. When we arrived at the house, the women were dressed in a way that said, "come get it." The woman I selected was young, maybe younger than my 18 years. She took me to her room and after the price was agreed upon, I believe it was five dollars, she began to undress me. After my pants and underpants were discarded, she had a bowl of warm water and she began to wash my privates.

As she washed me, I heard the noise of a baby in the corner behind a sheet on a clothesline that covered a baby and little girl about four or five years old. I stopped the woman and told her that I could not do this. She protested, and I told her that I was still going to pay her. In fact, I gave her double the money and thanked her for the time and left. This reminded me too much of my own life, and I did not want to morally compromise my own values, values that I had adopted as a result of an entirely new and positive information bank and value system. I never again put myself in such a position.

After advanced training, I was transferred to a
missile sight in Arlington Heights, Illinois. Again I
was placed in close quarters with a majority white
military population and from day one it was difficult. This was April of 1961 and the race wars of
the South were heating up. The *Brown v. Board of
Education* decision of 1954 and *Brown II* of 1955
were having an impact on the nation. Young
Black students' expectations, especially in the area
of education were in first gear. Demands for
admittance to research one and Ivy League universities and colleges arrived from every corner of
the Black population.

After I had pawned my trumpet and joined the
Army I used all of my spare time to read and
write. The poetry of Jean Toomer, Sterling A.
Brown, Langston Hughes, Margaret Walker, Arna
Bontemps and Melvin B. Tolson spoke directly

to my rising Black consciousness. However, it was the poetry of the Harlem Renaissance and Poet Renaissance that captured in me the possibility of becoming an activist/poet. I had started taking night courses, mainly English and Literature, at Crane Jr. College on Chicago's westside. We did not study any Black writers and when I asked why of the white instructors I usually received answers that implied acute ignorance and disrespect.

My last days in the United States Army were not good ones. However, my total Army experience was one that allowed me to grow and interact with people, mainly men, that were of other cultures and races. One fact about Americans is that they have all the "answers" to their own and other people's questions. Yet, very seldom do they contemplate the questions from the others.

I had arranged for an early release in order to attend Wilson Jr. College full time on the G.I. Bill. This was the summer of 1963, and the country was heating up due to the Black student rebellions of the south. I had grown impatient with the regimen and conformity of military life. I was 21, Black, unfree and willing to do anything to help in the on-going liberation struggles in the U.S. and Africa.

I was restless, angry at the country, yet deeply understood the raw power and arrogance of the rulership which was about to take us into a war in Southeast Asia. My exit from the Army was just months before President Kennedy and Johnson would try to save the Western world from Communism with napalm.

My poetry took on a new urgency.
On September 15, 1963, I wrote the poem
"Bloodsmiles." The significance of
"Bloodsmiles" is that it was written the day
before the bombing in Birmingham, Alabama
that shocked the world.

BLOODSMILES
(9/15/63 the day I left this society)

I remember the   time
when I could
smile—
smiles of
ignorance.
This was about
? years ago,
now—smiles do not
come as easily
as they are
supposed
to.
My smiles are
now fixed
and
come slowly
like the gradual
movement of tomatoes—
in a near empty
ketchup bottle—
about to be
eaten.

The U.S. Army taught me rather well to be a killer.
State killing was legal and encouraged. We never
practiced killing on white targets. It was the accu-
mulation of unlikeness, likeness, I mean, if it was
dark, shoot it. I left the military in August of 1963,
an early out to attend Chicago's Wilson Jr. College
on the G.I. Bill of Rights and to be recruited into
the national Black empowerment movements. On
September 16, the murder of four little Black girls
in Birmingham, Alabama confirmed in me the
rightness of my new direction. These children, our
children, were assassinated in their church praying
to a God who did not look like them. A great
many white people thought them evil and a communist threat to national security. I thought of
them as children, my cultural daughters, innocent,
without protection, loving and smiling, forgiving
and forever precious and promising. I took my
Army and life skills to the streets and along the way
became a poet.

—PART THREE—
Shaping Thoughts

Richard Wright

At fourteen I didn't quite put it so plainly, but I was certain that Richard Wright had altered my naïve and ignorant perception of the world of Black folks. Wright writes in *Black Boy*:

> At noon, when I was not running errands, I would join the rest of the Negroes in a little room at the front of the building overlooking the street. Here, in this underworld pocket of the building, we munched our lunches and discussed the ways of white folks toward Negroes. When two or more of us were talking, it was impossible for this subject not to come up. Each of us hated and feared the whites, yet had a white man put in a sudden appearance we would have assumed silent, obedient smiles. To our minds the white folks formed a kind of super-world: what was said by them during working hours was rehashed and weighed here; how they looked; what they wore; what moods they were in; on the job; who was getting fired and who was getting hired. But never once

did we openly say that we occupied none but subordinate positions in the building. Our talk was restricted to the petty relations, which formed the core of life for us. But under all our talk floated a latent sense of violence; the whites had drawn a line over which we dared not step and we accepted that line because our bread was at stake. But within our boundaries we, too, drew a line that included our right to bread regardless of the indignities or degradations involved in getting it. If a white man had sought to keep us from obtaining a job. Or enjoying the rights of citizenship, we would have bowed silently to his power. But if he had sought to deprive us of a dime, blood might have been spilt. Hence, our daily lives were so bound up with trivial objectives that to capitulate when challenged was tantamount to surrendering the right to life itself. Our anger was like the anger of children, passing quickly from one petty grievance to another, from the memory of one slight wrong to another.

There would be no turning back, Black cultural substance was exciting, liberating and stimulating. I was outraged at my own ignorance and complicity. Again, Richard Wright explains:

> It had been my accidental reading of fiction and literary criticism that had evoked in me vague glimpses of life's possibilities. Of course, I had never seen or met the men who wrote the books I read, and the kind of world in which they lived was as alien to me as the moon. But what enabled me to overcome my chronic distrust was that these books—written by men like Dreiser, Masters, Mencken, Anderson, and Lewis—seemed defensively critical of the straitened American environment. These writers seemed to feel that America could be shaped nearer to the hearts of those who lived in it. And it was out of these novels and stories and articles, out of the emotional impact of imaginative constructions of heroic or tragic deeds, that I felt touching my face a tinge of warmth from an unseen light; and in my leaving. I was groping

toward that invisible light, always trying to keep my face so set and turned that I would not lose the hope of its faint promise, using it as my justification for action.

The white South said that it knew "niggers," and I was what the white South called a "nigger." Well, the white South had never known me—never known what I thought, what I felt. The white South said that I had a "place" in life. Well, I had never felt my "place"? or, rather, my deepest instincts had always made me reject the "place" to which the white South had assigned me. It had never occurred to me that I was in any way an inferior being. And no word that I had ever heard fall from the lips of southern white men had ever made me really doubt the worth of my own humanity. True, I had lied. I had stolen. I had struggled to contain my seething anger. I had fought. And it was perhaps a mere accident that I had never killed...But in what other ways had the South allowed me to be natural, to be real, to be myself, except in rejection, rebellion, and aggression? Not only had the southern whites not known me, but, more important still, as I had lived in the South I had not had the chance to learn who I was.

Reading Wright, if nothing else, forced me to confront the question, Who am I? The question would beat me all of my young life. Black, the color in the national consciousness was still not beautiful. Most of my people, including me, either hated our own selves, or at best were acutely ambivalent about the positive aspect of being "Black."

Reading Richard Wright's *Black Boy* was like victim B and C to a nutrient-deficient body raised primarily on canned vegetables, fast food, junk food and sugary beverages. For example, I drank more pop and kool-aid than water; obviously not understanding the short term or lasting damage that poor nutrition has on the physical and mental development of all people. Fortunately, I read *Black Boy* at a very impressionable age, and it foisted in me questions that encouraged one to seek out everything that Richard Wright had published.

After reading Wright's *Uncle Tom's Children*, *12 Million Black Voices*, and *Native Son*, I realized the deep poverty, coupled with an embarrassing ignorance with which I, my family, and Black people lived. Common sense demanded rather forcefully and clearly that the one weapon that could help alleviate some of our pain and complicity is knowledge. Wright's essay "The Psychological Reactions of Oppressed People" in *White Man, Listen!* introduced me to the new world of psychology and gave me an insightful look at myself from a scientific and philosophical world view. He called it the "Frog Perspectives":

> This is a phrase I've borrowed from Nietzsche to describe someone looking from below upward, a sense of someone who feels himself lower than others. The concept of distance involved here is not physical; it is psychological. It involves a situation in which, for moral or social reasons, a person or a group feels that there is another person or group above it. Yet, physically, they all live on the same general material plane. A certain degree of hate combined with love (ambivalence) is always involved in

> this looking from below upward and
> the object against which the subject is
> measuring himself undergoes constant
> change. He loves the object because
> he would like to resemble it; he hates
> the object because his chances of
> resembling it are remote, slight.

Wright made me aware of the socialization and acculturation of Black people. Prior to reading him, I was ill-informed about the class differences among Black folk. We were urban poor, and I came from southern poorer. All I knew was that we were all in the same sinking boat, and there were few life rafts thrown to us. Wright is death on the "Negro" middle class who, without too much thought or consideration, tried to "ape" the white people whenever possible, especially in their presence.

In *White Man, Listen!*, I was introduced to Africa in a way that was not embarrassing or belittling for the first time in my young life. You must remember that my generation grew up with images of Africa that were quite deadly and effective. Africa to us was Tarzan, Jungle Jim, She-woman and where the only purpose of African men and women was to serve white people. When we were not serving, worshipping, imitating, admiring and desiring to be like white people, we were involved in activities that stated, in no uncertain terms, that we hated ourselves. This self-hatred was translated in our rooting for Tarzan or any other whites in their battles against the Black "savage," the Black "beasts," or any African that had an ounce of self-respect. In our embracing of white supremacy, we did not realize that our riding with the Lone Ranger and Tonto against the many nations of indigenous people of the Americas who had been renamed Indians, that we subconsciously wanted to be white and powerful. However, after reading and re-reading Wrights', "The 'Whiteness' of the White World," "Who and What is a 'Savage'?," "The Suspicion of 'Stupidity'," "Acting," "Ideology as Intimacy," "Flight into The Past," "Lay Priests," "The Zone of Silence" and other mental bullets from *White Man, Listen!* did I really begin to understand the unique and awesome power of words, the magic of language, the effectiveness of a writer at his best.

I grew almost over night into a person that questioned everything and everybody. Wright pushed my young mind into a world where less than eight percent of the world's population rule as if the majority of Asians, Africans, poor

Europeans and other non-whites existed only for their benefit. To me and others, whiteness had become the impossible standard. This was why we bleached our skin, processed our hair, pinched our noses and talked (when mis-educated) like something was stuck up our asses. Wright's words hit like hammers, and they needed to if he was going to have any affect on brain-washed minds, like mine, that seemed to live for the weekend and physical pleasure. Again Richard Wright gives us his insight:

> Who says that we black men must duplicate and ape the development of the white man? Aren't we in the position of studying the white man's mistakes, taking advantage of them, and making even faster progress than he made? To imitate the white man means that we are still slaves in our hearts.
>
> I say, let us be free; and freedom means mapping out our own road for ourselves, making our own mistakes and being responsible for them.

Now I began to realize that Little Rock and Detroit were really foreign territories that were recently conquered by Europeans, who committed genocide against the "Indians" and raped Africa of its people, transported us to the west to work the land—that the Indians refused to—to create wealth, which translated into power for white folks. This was the real cycle of white empowerment. Control the land, and you control the people. Wright's essay "The Literature of the Negro in the United States," opened up the value and wisdom of Black literature for me. He introduced me to the concept of *culture* and by association the concept of *acculturation*. He writes:

> But there were some few Negroes who, through luck, diligence, and courage, did rise and make the culture of their nation their own even though that nation still rejected them; and, having made the culture of their nation their own, they hurled pleading words against the deaf ears of white America until the very meaning of their lives came to be in telling how and what the rejection which their country leveled against them made

them feel. You remember the Greek legend of Narcissus who was condemned by Nemesis to fall in love with his own reflection which he saw in the water of a fountain? Well, the middle-class Negro writers were condemned by America to stand before a Chinese Wall and wail that they were like other men, that they felt as others felt. It is this relatively static stance of emotion that I call The Narcissistic Level. These Negroes were in every respect the equal of whites; they were valid examples of personality types of Western culture; but they lived in a land where even insane white people were counted above them. They were men whom constant rejection had rendered impacted of feeling, choked of emotion. During the first quarter of this century, these men, Trotter, DuBois, Washington, etc., fought as the Negro had never fought before for equal rights, but they fought in vain. It is true that when their voices reached the ears of many philanthropic whites, they did win a few concessions which helped

185

Negro institutions to exist. But the irony in the efforts of these Negroes was that the gains they won fastened ever tighter around their necks the shackles of Jim Crowism. For example, every new hospital, clinic, and school that was built was a Negro hospital, a Negro clinic, a Negro school! So, though Negroes were slowly rising out of their debased physical conditions, the black ghettos were growing ever larger; instead of racial segregation lessening, it grew, deepened, spread.

Wright gave me an entirely different interpretation of Black spirituals and blues, two folk arts that helped our people to survive and develop. He conveyed in the essay examples of Black music as a rebellious, comforting and fight-back art. He put literature into a social, cultural and political context. He created a literature that worked for a people, rather than against a people. It was Wright who introduced me to Phyllis Wheatley, Claude McKay, Booker T. Washington, W.E.B. DuBois, Monroe Trotter, Countee Cullen, Frank Horne, Arna Bontemps, Langston Hughes, Frank Marshall Davis, Melvin

B. Tolson, Sterling A. Brown, Margaret Walker, Gwendolyn Brooks, Robert E. Hayden, Chester Himes, Ralph Ellison, Ann Petry, Frank Yerby, James Baldwin and other Black writers and poets.

Richard Wright's *12 Million Black Voices: A Folk History of the Negro in The United States,* with photo-direction by Edwin Rossi, painted America in words and photographs that were an unmistakably clear and unambiguous portrait of an enslaved but unbroken people, my people. His analysis of the South and the North helped, as did *Black Boy,* put my life into an economic and a political context. I now realized that the acute poverty that I and my family endured was not because we were, by nature, inferior or incompetent, but that we had become pawns in a much larger geo-political, economic war of white nationalism and imperialism. It was Wright who taught me that we traded the bosses of the fields for the bosses of the Urban tenaments and work-places.

After reading Wright's *Uncle Tom's Children,* and *Native Son,* I had become a stranger in my own home and neighborhood. Suddenly, there was no one to talk to. None of my teachers, all white, had read or ever heard of Richard Wright. Not one of the Blacks in my limited circle of friends and family knew of his work except my mother. My mother was not a highly or formally educated woman; however, she did read. She also introduced me to the works of Chester Himes. Himes and Wright were entering popular culture, and their books became points of argument and discussions. She had a copy of his *Cast the First Stone*, a novel about prison life. Himes in his unique writing style vividly captured life inside the nation's prisons. Himes writes of the brutality of a life with its own rules, taboos and rituals. This was the first book that I read that covered homosexuality and how it played out in a world without women. Clearly, after reading Himes, prison was a place I didn't want to go.

Paul Robeson

The destruction of my copy of *Here I Stand* during my basic training served as a clear indicator that Paul Robeson's writing would stay on my reading list—no matter what the cost.

Paul Robeson was a man of extraordinary talent, cultural knowledge, fearlessness, physical and mental strength, warmth and magnetism. He, like W.E.B. DuBois and Langston Hughes, had been abused by the House Sub-Committee on Un-American Activity. However, it was Robeson who was one of the first Black men to become an international film and stage star.

His baritone voice enshrined him into the hearts of most of the world's people who heard him. He used his international prestige to fight for the human rights of all people. However, it was his birth nation, the United States, that hounded and persecuted him the most viciously. Robeson as a stage and film actor was able to use his fame and money to fight for the abused, oppressed poor and underclass worldwide. The white supremacists of this land, especially those in Congress, hated and feared his voice of liberation. The right wing promotion of the Cold War viewed the Soviet Union as the ungodly enemy of the West and the United States in particular.

Even though the U.S. and the USSR were allies during World War II, the policy maker in this country immediately before the end of the war directed its war machine—the Pentagon war department and State Department—to make ready for the almost certain confrontation with Russia and its confederated states. Paul Robeson was loved in the USSR. The people embraced him as an artist, truth teller and human rights activist. Because of this and his outspoken voice on behalf of his people, he was "white listed," forced to appear before the House Sub-Committee on Un-American Activity where, true to his history, he went on the attack rather than sit quietly and be accused by the real criminals of this earth. He attacked his accusers and did not kowtow to the committee or anyone else. Mr. Robeson, who was clearly one of the wealthiest Black men in America and as the most visible advocate for his people's freedom was seen by the ruling white elite as someone who had to be broken. They tried and failed.

I was only twelve years old when the Supreme Court ruled in favor of Brown in *Brown v. Board of Education.* However, I immediately recognized its importance in my own school. As a paperboy at that time, I read and reread the angry reactions by many of the country's leaders

to the decision. However, Robeson, like DuBois
continued to fight for the rights of Blacks.
Robeson writes in *Here I Stand*:

> As I see it, the challenge which today
> confronts the Negro people in the
> United States can be stated in two
> propositions:
>
> 1. Freedom can be ours, here
> and now: the long-sought goal
> of full citizenship under the
> Constitution is now within our
> reach.
> 2. We have the power to
> achieve that goal: what we our-
> selves do will be decisive.
>
> These two ideas are strongly denied or
> seriously doubted by many in our
> land, and the denial and doubt are
> demonstrated both by action and
> inaction in the crisis of our time. Let
> me begin by discussing the first
> proposition. Those who are openly
> our enemies—the avowed upholders
> of the myth of White Supremacy—
> have bluntly stated their position on

the matter: Not now and not ever shall the Jim Crow system be abolished. "Let me make this clear," declared Eastland, the foremost spokesman for this group, in a Senate speech ten days after the Supreme Court outlawed school segregation, "the South will retain segregation." And the strength of this viewpoint was shown when a hundred other Senators and Representatives from the South signed a manifesto in which they denounced the Court's decision and pledged that they would resist its enforcement. The whole world has seen how these defiant words have become defiant deeds. Others, who claim to be our friends, insist that the immediate enforcement of our lawful rights is not possible. We must wait, we are told, until the hearts of those who persecute us have softened—until Jim Crow dies of old age. This idea is called "Gradualism." It is said to be a practical and constructive way to achieve the blessings of democracy for colored Americans. But the idea itself is but another form of race discrimination: in no other area of our society are lawbreakers granted an indefinite time to comply with the provisions of law. There is nothing in the 14th and 15th Amendments, the legal guarantees of our full citizenship rights, which says that the Constitution is to be enforced "gradually" where Negroes are concerned. "Gradualism" is a mighty long road. It stretches back 100 long and weary years, and looking forward it has no end. Long before Emancipation was won, our people had learned that the promises of freedom in the future could not be trusted, and the folk—knowledge was put down in the bitter humor of this song from slavery days:

> My old master promised me
> when he died he'd set me free,
> he lived so long that his head got
> bald and he gave up the notion of
> dying at all.

Well, chattel slavery was finally abolished—not gradually but all at once. The slave-masters were never converted to liberal philosophy: they were crushed by the overwhelming force that was brought to bear against their rotten system. They were not asked to give up, penny by penny, the billions of dollars they owned in human property: the 13th Amendment took it all away in an instant.

These remarks are from the chapter "The Time is Now." I cannot overly emphasize the importance of Paul Robeson to Black people and people of goodwill worldwide. He was the youngest of six children of a father-preacher who had formerly been enslaved. Fighting through Jim Crowism, racial discrimination and poverty, he eventually graduated in the top five percent of his undergraduate and law school classes. His natural intelligence, his "Nubian Prince" looks, his wonderland baritone voice soon brought him to the attention of the professional theatre, motion pictures, the concert stage and the world.

During the rise of Nazism and Fascism in Europe and due to his highly unusual visibility and consciousness, he began to speak out for justice and equality for the millions of refugees coming to America and dispersed throughout Europe. Robeson saw quite rightly in the struggles of Jews, Gypsies, and all non-Aryan people that their fight was the same that Black people fought in their land of birth.

It was now clear to him that White Supremacy was truly an international problem and that an awareness of the politics and economics of race and color in which he grew up was now playing big-death worldwide. He gave of himself, time, money, benefit concerts, speeches, the use of his name, special time away from his family and much more. And for that, this country took his passport, forbade him to travel, disrupted his concerts in the United States and initiated a well-planned campaign of character assassination against him.

Yet, as his money dried up, as friend and foe turned on him, he maintained a dignity and battle face that never allowed anyone to state that he was broken or beaten. His is the courage I learned from. It was Paul Robeson who set the standard for me of an engaged artist willing to put everything on the line for truth and justice. He remains a hero in my heart. His words, his endurance in the face of unimaginable evil helped me survive the United States Army.

The Re-Education of a Negro

Much of my reading about Black people was included in the comprehensive anthology, *The Negro Caravan*, edited by Sterling A. Brown of Howard University, Arthur P. Davis of Virginia Union University and Ulysses Lee of Lincoln University, published by The Dryden Press of New York in 1941. I found a first edition in mint condition at a used library book sale in 1958 in Detroit. A week before enlisting in the U.S. Army, in a used bookstore in St. Louis, I found a copy of *The Poetry of the Negro* edited by the great poets Langston Hughes and Arna Bontemps. I can't begin to clearly write of the joy in finding the two anthologies. The books literally opened me up to the enormous world of Black literature. *The Negro Caravan*, with its clear and knowledgeable introductions to each section: Short Stories, Novel (excerpts), Poetry, Folk Literature, Drama, Biography and Autobiography, Essays: Historical, Social, Cultural and Personal Reflections, gave me a pathway into Black literature that was almost unattainable for the lay reader at that time. *The Poetry of the Negro* gave me a survey course in international poetry. The poets Hughes and

Bontemps included in this major anthology are from the United States, primarily Black, but a few whites like Walt Whitman, Stephen Vincent Bene't, Hart Crane, Carl Sandburg, Muriel Rukeyser, Karl Shapiro and others; poets from the Caribbean, British Guiana, British Honduras, Barbados, Trinidad, Haiti, Martinique, Cuba and Africa are also included. This anthology took me on a trip that accented Black poets of the U.S., but also allowed me to sample the works of Aime Cesaire, Nicolas Guillen, Leon Damas, and Claude McKay.

The poets whose works influenced me the greatest were Langston Hughes, Robert Hayden, Margaret Walker, Frank Marshall Davis, Waring Cuney, Sterling A. Brown, Melvin B. Tolson, Arna Bontemps, Gwendolyn Brooks, and Claude McKay. It was McKay's poem "If We Must Die" that proved to me that art in the form of a poem can fight the right battles:

> If we must die, let it not be like hogs
> Hunted and penned in an inglorious spot,
> While round us bark the mad and hungry dogs,
> Making their mock at our accursed lot.
> If we must die, O let us nobly die,
> So that our precious blood may not be shed

In vain; then even the monsters we defy
Shall be constrained to honor us though dead!
O kinsmen! We must meet the common foe!
Though far outnumbered let us show us brave,
And for their thousand blows deal one deathblow!
What though before us lies the open grave?
Like men we'll face the murderous, cowardly pack,
Pressed to the wall, dying, but fighting back!

Also, Margaret Walker's "For My People," Frank Marshall Davis' "Robert Whitmore," Waring Cuney's "No Images," Robert E. Hayden's "Runagate Runagate" and "Frederick Douglass," and Gwendolyn Brooks' "Kitchenette Building" and her insightful "Of DeWitt Williams on His Way to Lincoln Cemetery" reprinted here:

He was born in Alabama.
He was bred in Illinois.
He was nothing but a
Plain black boy.
Swing low swing low sweet
sweet chariot.
Nothing but a plain black boy.

Drive him past the Pool Hall.
Drive him past the Show.
Blind within his casket,
But maybe he will know.

Down through Forty-seventh Street:
Underneath the L,
And-Northwest Corner, Prairie,
That he loved so well.

Don't forget the Dance Halls-
Warwick and Savoy,
Where he picked his women, where
He drank his liquid joy.

Born in Alabama.
Bred in Illinois.
He was nothing but a
Plain black boy.

Swing low swing low sweet
sweet chariot.
Nothing but a plain black boy.

The reason Black poets were so important in my maturation was that they were not afraid to confront the problems of our people in a language that was umbiguous and on fire. As with the first two and last two stanzas of Margaret Walkers' prose-poem, "For My People":

For my people everywhere singing their slave songs
    repeatedly: their dirges and their ditties and their blues
    and jubilees, praying their prayers nightly to an
    unknown god, bending their knees humbly to an
    unseen power;

For my people lending their strength to the years, to the
    gone years and the now years and the maybe years,
    washing ironing cooking scrubbing sewing mending
    hoeing plowing digging planting pruning patching
    dragging along never gaining never reaping never
    knowing and never understanding;
. . . .
For my people standing staring trying to fashion a better way
    from confusion, from hypocrisy and misunderstanding,
    trying to fashion a world that will hold all the people,
    all the faces, all the adams and eves and their countless
    generations;

Let a new earth rise. Let another world be born. Let a
bloody peace be written in the sky. Let a second
generation full of courage issue forth; let a people
loving freedom come to growth. Let a beauty full of
healing and a strength of final clenching be the pulsing
in our spirits and our blood. Let the martial songs be
written, let the dirges disappear. Let a race of men now
rise and take control.

The poem is a battle cry to resist and develop.
All the poets mentioned were to play a large role
in my development as a poet. I would eventually
meet Bontemps, Brown, Walker, Hayden, and
Ms. Brooks—who was to ultimately influence me
like no other person, poet or writer. There are
other writers and poets who helped me to endure
the military without losing too much of my
mind. However, along with Richard Wright and
Langston Hughes, it would be Arna Bontemps,
Sterling Brown, Margaret Walker, Robert
Hayden and Gwendolyn Brooks who I would
read and study as if my life depended upon their
words and art.

W.E.B. DuBois

Like that of Richard Wright, Chester Himes, Langston Hughes and Paul Robeson, the works of W.E.B. DuBois impacted my early life. As a poor boy raised on the lower east side of Detroit, Michigan, the words of DuBois and Robeson often peppered the conversations of Black workers from the Ford and General Motors plants who frequented our church and neighborhood. Both of them were intimately involved in progressive politics and labor movements in the 1940s and 1950s.

However, it was not until 1957, at the very impressionable age of fifteen, after reading Richard Wright's *White Man, Listen!* and E. Franklin Frazier's *Black Bourgeosie* that the name W.E.B. DuBois took on a kind of intellectual urgency. Both Wright and Frazier quoted DuBois as if he were the authority. Frazier writes in *Black Bourgeosie*, "W.E.B. DuBois, who became the editor of the *Crisis*, the official organ of The National Association for the Advancement of Colored People, was the leader of the militant Negro." The word militant sent me running to the Public Library to read *Crisis* Magazine.

It was not until 1960, upon reading Paul
Robeson's *Here I Stand* and his quoting
from *The Souls of Black Folks* that I began
systematically to read W.E.B. DuBois on my
own. I was in the United States Army, the poor
boys answer to full employment, where the
slogan "hurry up and wait" took on a different
meaning for me. I waited with books in my
hands, backpack and pockets.   I read and
re-read, studied the history and culture of Black
people, and extended my study into the areas of
political economy.

DuBois had already articulated that the
problem of the twentieth century would be
"race." As I studied his work, I began to see
possibilities for myself for two reasons: (1)
DuBois was a high-yellow Black man (as am I)
who had devoted his life to the un-compromising
development and liberation of Black people; and
(2) his writing represented liberating medicine
and intellectual energy for my young mind. All
of DuBois' work, whether in sociology, history,
politics, fiction, or poetry, led to the reconstruction of the Black mind. The passage that both
freed me intellectually and gave meaning to the
rage that continued to tear me apart came from
The Souls of Black Folk:

After the Egyptian and Indian, the Greek and Roman, the Teuton and Mongolian, the Negro is a sort of seventh son, born with a veil, and gifted with second sight in this American world—a world which yields him no true self-consciousness, but only lets him see himself through the revelation of the other world. It is a peculiar sensation, this double-consciousness, this sense of always looking at one's self through the eyes of others, of measuring one's soul by the tape of a world that looks on in amused contempt and pity. One ever feels his twoness—an American, a Negro; two souls, two thoughts, two unreconciled strivings; two warring ideals in one dark body, whose dogged strength alone keeps it from being torn asunder.

The history of the American Negro is the history of this strife—this longing to attain self-conscious manhood, to merge his double self into a better and truer self. In this merging he wishes neither of the older selves to be lost. He would not Africanize America, for America has too much to teach the world and Africa. He would not bleach his Negro soul in a flood of white Americanism, for he knows that Negro blood has a message for the world. He simply wishes to make it possible for a man to be both a Negro and an American, without being cursed and spit upon by his fellows, without having the doors of Opportunity closed roughly in his face.

Yes, I knew that I was different and Black. However, it was DuBois' analysis that brought me to where I could appreciate and begin to reconcile the different "selves" in me. Color and psychology, color and history, color and enslavement, color and politics, color and economics, color and culture, color and rage, took on new meanings for me. I came to understand that the white images and symbols that assigned me to certain roles in life had nothing to do with the quality and content of my history or my mind. My search for authenticity was being led by the literature of W.E.B. DuBois and others.

DuBois' *Black Reconstruction* and *The World and Africa* were two books that ultimately un-locked my mind and gave form to my own thoughts in the area of Black history. DuBois was a Black intellectual who remained true to his calling in that he not only wrote and documented history, he, by his actions, via the NAACP (National Association for the Advancement of Colored People) and other progressive organizations, tried to impact and change the world, as an intellectual, scholar, editor, Pan-Africanist and activist. He went to his grave in Ghana in 1963, at the age of ninety-five, never giving in to the long and comfortable compromises. DuBois was a political scholar, leader, creative genius and activist for "life."

As a young man, I was fascinated with the breath and scope of DuBois' writings. He personified for me the essence of the engaged Black intellectual: scholarly, culturally informed, politically active, institution builder, teacher and deep thinker or what some would call a philosopher. He states it best in his private diary where on his twenty-fifth birthday he noted "I am striving to make my life all that life may be...God knows that I am sorely puzzled...the general proposition of working for the world's good too soon becomes sickly sentimentality. I therefore tell the world that the unknown lay in my hands and work for the rise of the Negro people, taking for granted that their best development means the best development of the world."

Most critical and serious readers are aware of DuBois the sociologist, political scientist, historian, editor, human rights activist and Pan-Africanist, but there is little written about DuBois the creative writer or poet. In his *The Gift of Black Folk* he predated Black Studies by fifty years by surveying the numerous contributions of Black people in the making of America. For me as a young writer trying to find a voice this book was just as important as *The Souls of Black Folk* because he covered the landscape of the Black experience from Black explorers, laborers, soldiers to "The Freedom of Womanhood." His chapter on "Negro Art and Literature" opened the door just a bit wider for my inquisitive mind:

The Negro is primarily an artist. The usual way of putting this is to speak disdainfully of his "sensuous" nature. This means that the only race which has held at bay the life destroying forces of the tropics, has gained there from in some slight compensation a sense of beauty, particularly for sound and color, which characterizes the race. The Negro blood which flowed in the veins of many of the mightiest of the Pharaohs accounts for much of Egyptian art, and indeed Egyptian civilization owes much in its origin to the development of the large strain of Negro blood which manifested itself in every grade of Egyptian society.

Today, our language is more culturally directed and one's genetic code is more specific and accurate than one's blood line. We understand that Dr. DuBois' life mission was the political, economic and spiritual liberation of his people coupled with the intellectual development and maturation of all oppressed people. This objective still resonates in the hearts, minds and souls of true intellectuals, activist and artist everywhere. The questions that committed persons continually ask themselves is, "How does one approach the breadth and scope of a DuBois?"

Few scholars or readers are aware of DuBois' fiction and poetry. His novels *The Quest of the "Silver Fleece"* and *Dark Princess: A Romance* were not best sellers and generally did not receive favorable reviews. He was encouraged to write fiction by his editor after the phenomenal success of *The Souls of Black Folk*. According to Herbert Aptheker, the distinguished historian and executor of DuBois' papers, *The Quest of the Silver Fleece* remains an interesting effort at a realistic portrayal of the impact of cotton, racism and peonage upon the nation early in the twentieth century, as Upton Sinclair and Frank Norris had done about the same time with meat and wheat." Dr. DuBois' collection *Darkwater: Voices From Within The Veil*, part autobiography, journalism, fiction and poetry—first published in 1920 just beyond his fiftieth birthday, displayed in a single volume a seminal mind of the twentieth century as well as a highly competent creative writer. In fact, in 1901 he wrote "A Litany At Atlanta," a poetic prayer about the Atlanta race riot which is his most published work.

However, it was in the pages of _The Crisis_ magazine, the official organ of the NAACP, where his dedication and commitment to literature is clearly documented. As the founding editor of _The Crisis,_ in 1910, he finally had a publication where he could not only advocate for the rights of his people, provide a forum for creative and non-fiction writers, but also let loose each month the fired up essays for which his education and culture had prepared him. _The Crisis_ at its zenith had a readership and "listenership" of over one hundred thousand, which in itself was phenomenal considering that less than fifteen per cent of the Black population in America could read or write in 1910. Therefore, family members, ministers, and professional Black folks who could read-read to those who couldn't. A reading base of one hundred thousand today easily translates into over one million. According to Reverend Howard Melish, _The Crisis_ went every month into one-tenth of the Negro homes of the entire nation. Rev. Melish also writes:

> _The Crisis_ combined literary quality and broad popular appeal. DuBois devised all kinds of contests with prizes for poems, short stores, essays,

one act dramas, pictures of the prettiest Negro baby or the high school or college graduate currently receiving the most significant academic honor. With the aid of one secretary who could type, and writing most of his letters long hand himself, he conducted a mountainous correspondence in search of manuscripts, pictures, and artwork for the covers, acknowledging the contributions accepted and explaining those returned, lest the senders be discouraged. In this manner, he discovered and encouraged two generations of Negro poets, writers, dramatists and artists. The one-act plays that appeared in "Crisis" were made available at a modest royalty for presentation in churches, schools and fraternal lodges, in an endeavor to create a Negro theatre.

Among the hundreds of creative writers featured monthly in the pages of *The Crisis* were poets Gwendolyn Bennett, Arna Bontemps, William Stanley Braithwaite, Sterling Brown, Countee Cullen, Allison Davis, Jessie Fauset,

Frank Horne, Langston Hughes, James Weldon Johnson, Claude McKay and Jean Toomer. Fiction writers included Charles W. Chesnutt, Jesse Fauset, Rudolph Fisher, Fenton Johnson, and others. DuBois' devotion to literature is also displayed in the hundreds of book reviews he wrote and published in journals and newspapers as diverse as *The New Republic*, *The Nation*, *International Herald Tribune*, *Phylon*, *New York Post*, and of course, *The Crisis*.

Dr. DuBois' Selected Poems was published in 1963 in Accra, Ghana by Ghana University Press. At the request and invitation of the Honorable Kwame Nkrumah, President of Ghana, Dr. DuBois and his second wife, Shirley Graham DuBois, also a serious writer, had set up residence in Ghana in part to complete his works on the Encyclopedia Africana. He and Shirley Graham DuBois also moved to escape continued harassment in the United States, where under the "Red" scare he had been hounded and persecuted by the U.S. Government and the press for his outspoken views and ideas on the liberation of his people and oppressed people of the world. His being in the forefront of the International Peace and Pan African movements also positioned him as a marked man. These were the days of the "Cold War" between the United

States and the USSR and DuBois, Langston
Hughes, Paul Robeson and other progressive
Blacks and whites lived under constant harass-
ment from their "own" government.

As a poet, he brought to his art the same
thought, care, diligence and discipline that
infused his other works. As in much of the
poetry published at that time, DuBois writes in
rhyme and a somewhat strict metrical pattern.
Yet, much of his poetry is in free verse, where the
meter is more internal to the poem itself. These
poems are more fluid and the rhythms are more
evident and organic. It is clear that a lifelong
social conscience flavors most of his poetry,
produced early in his writing career. There is in
many of the poems a deep, deep belief in God
and God's ability to order the world. DuBois'
devotion to Black people is unquestioned and
many of the poems are pro-children and anti-war
as in this excerpt from "WAR":

Save the children and their dreams
Save the color and the sound
Save the form of faiths unfound

Save Civilization soul and sod,
Save the tattered shreds of God!
War is murder, murder hate

And suicide, stupidity
Incorporate.

In 1912, DuBois published in *The Crisis* "The Riddle of the Sphinx," where his biting anger and total disillusionment with the white world and its almost global colonization of Africa and other nations of color invited these lines:

All the dirt of London,
All the scum of New York;
Valiant spoilers of women
And conquerors of unarmed men;
Shameless breeders of bastards,
Drunk with the greed of gold,
Baiting their blood-stained hooks

With cant for the souls of the simple
Bearing the white man's burden
Of liquor and lust and lies!

Unthankful we wince in the East,
Unthankful we wail from the westward,
Unthankfully thankful, we curse,
In the unworn wastes of the wild:

I hate them, Oh!
I hate them well,

I hate them, Christ!
As I hate hell!
If I were God,
I'd sound their knell
This day!

Well, these are not the words of most of today's "public intellectuals" who are too timid or frightened to express the anger and feelings of a great many of their people and other oppressed people's of the world. "In Children of the Moon," first published in *Darkwater* in 1920, he passionately writes against the oppression of women and children. His eye is always on escaping one's ugly and depressing conditions, seeking liberation and a lasting freedom:

Wings, wings, eternal wings,
'Til the hot, red blood,
Flood fleeing flood,
Thundered through heaven and mine ears,
While all across a purple sky,
The last vast pinion
Trembled to unfold.

I rose upon the Mountain of the Moon,—
I felt the blazing glory of the Sun:
I heard the Song of Children crying, "Free!"

I saw the face of Freedom—
And I died.

One of the last poems written by Dr. DuBois was "Ghana Calls," dedicated to Osagyefo Kwame Nkrumah and published in the influential journal, *Freedomways* in February of 1962:

> Enslaved the Black and killed the Red
> And armed the Rich to loot the Dead;
> Worshipped the whores of Hollywood
> Where once the Virgin Mary stood
> And lynched the Christ.
>
> Awake, awake, O sleeping world
> Honor the sun;
> Worship the stars, those vaster suns
>
> Who rule the night.
> Where black is bright
> And all unselfish work is right
> And Greed is sin.
> And Africa leads on:
> Pan Africa!

On February 23, 1962, DuBois turned ninety-four years old (we share the same birth date). He was almost a century old and still productive. This says a great deal about a mind and spirit that has been employed in intellectual and liberation studies and actions for over seventy-five years. As the saying goes "use it or lose it."

My favorite poem of DuBois, which I will quote in its entirety, is "The Song Of The Smoke" first published in *The Horizon* in 1899. The power of the poem again speaks to the freedom of the smoke king and Black people's liberating journey:

> I am the smoke king,
> I am black.
> I am swinging in the sky,
> I am ringing worlds on high;
> I am the thought of the throbbing mills,
> I am the ripple of trading rills,
> Up I'm curling from the sod,
> I am whirling home to God.
> I am the smoke king,
> I am black.
> I am the smoke king,
> I am black.
> I am wreathing broken hearts,
> I am sheathing devils' darts;

Dark inspiration of iron times,
Wedding the toil of toiling climes
Shedding the blood of bloodless crimes,
Down I lower in the blue,
Up I tower toward the true,
I am the smoke king,
I am black.
I am the smoke king,
I am black.
I am the smoke king,
I am black.
I am darkening with song,
I am hearkening to wrong;
I will be black as blackness can,
The blacker the mantle the mightier
the man,
My purpling midnights no day dawn
may ban.
I am carving God in night,
I am painting hell in white.

I am the smoke king,
I am black.
I am the smoke king,
I am black.
I am cursing ruddy morn,
I am nursing hearts unborn;
Souls unto me are as mists in the night,

I whiten my blackmen, I blacken my white,
What's the hue of a hide to a man in his
might!
Hail, the, grilly, grimy hands,
Sweet Christ, pity toiling lands!
Hail to the smoke king,
Hail to the black!

This dynamic first person poem is a thundering call to Black consciousness sixty-six years prior to the Black Arts Movement of the 1960s and 1970s. DuBois was just twenty-one years old and ready to fight for the social and political rights of his people. His use of language that called us back to Black predates the poets of the Harlem Renaissance, the post depression writers and, of course, the writers of the Black Arts Movement of the sixties. DuBois understood the power of poetic language, carefully used words, the disarming affect of poems that danced and played like notes from the horns of Louis Armstrong and Charlie Parker. The scholar and critic Arnold Rampersad has written that the "Song of The Smoke" is perhaps the first Afro-American poem of this kind...that is "purely celebrational of the Black man." And, it was undoubtedly clear, few writers used the language to celebrate Black people as well as and as often as DuBois. The language of Black people excited me, taking on new meanings and urgencies. That which is most unique about us, other than the infinite variety of our facial expressions and skin shading, is the musical quality of our utterances. We speak in magical voices. Whether we are from Harlem or Senegal, Nigeria or Detroit, Los Angeles or Kenya, Jamaica or London, Rio de Janeiro or Panama.

We bring to language its beat, it cadences, its walking rhythms, its stops and goes, its skips and its balances; we add style and substance to whatever language in which we communicate, dance, or sing. There is an African or Black side of most languages. Language is cultural. Our language is our name.

It became increasingly clear to me that Blacks in America, specifically North America, USA, sing or speak an African American Black English. The musical quality of Black voices help to define the regions of the country in which one is reared. Our voices carry our villages. There is a Northern, Southern and Western voice. There are Mississippi, New York, Cleveland, St. Louis, and San Francisco sounds radiating from the Blackside of life. Our language carries our history. It is memories being vocalized. All cultures, all people have this. Blacks in this country have been negatively categorized, stigmatized, and put down by others, mainly whites, who are ignorant about the value and beauty of cultural and linguistic differences. The blues is our language; it is our indigenous fiction, short stories that swing and for me, this literature was grounding me in a culture that was exciting and life giving.

Black vocal harmonies have influenced the world. From the scatting of Louis Armstrong, Ella Fitzgerald, and Dizzy Gillespie to the distinctiveness of Lou Rawls and Aretha Franklin, to the phrasing of Joe Williams, Billie Holiday, and Nancy Wilson to the rooted-ness of B.B. King and Bessie Smith. Black vocal groups put the wop in do-wop, introducing three, four, five, and six-part harmony. The Memphis, Mississippi, and Chicago blues are internationally acclaimed. Urban rap, which sprang from the folk songs and spirituals of Black folks, influences young people across the globe. The political and social content of the best of Black rap is directly connected to the liberating poetry of the 1960s, which proclaimed loud and clear that America was in deep, deep trouble, raging out of control on an

anti-Black/anti-people course, and not to be
trusted or depended upon. My questions about
our existence became more focused and political.

I now understood that many African
Americans of my generation received their
intellectual substance, beauty, memories, and
bonding traditions from the language of Black
writers and poets. The Langston Hughes, Zora
Neale Hurston and W.E.B. DuBois in each of us
is unique. They and we took the voices of the
church, streets, fields, factories, clubs, offices,
homes, projects, playgrounds, locker rooms,
restaurants, bedrooms, after-hours joints, hotels,
schools and colleges, trains and buses, and placed
them in a Colored American, Negro American,
Black American, and today's African American
context. The Brookses, Wests, Larsens,
Wheatleys, Walkers, McKays, Toomers, Haydens,
Tolsons, Bontemps, Browns, Wrights, Ellisons,
Davises, Hortons, Douglasses, Cullens,
Hansberrys, Johnsons, Hornes, Woodsons,
Dunbars, Himeses, Baldwins, Killens, Bennetts,
Garveys, DuBoises and countless other writers
and poets reached into the souls of Black folks
and humanized our pain, joy, suffering, achieve-
ments, incompetence, goodness, short and long
comings for the world to hear, read, and
hopefully understand and grow from. To read,

study and write in the tradition of African American literature is, in itself, enough work for hundreds of serious Ph.D. programs and the works of W.E.B. DuBois would be at the core of such programs.

I learned to not apologize to anyone for the language of Black folks in America. Our language, our voices, are not only legitimate, but right and necessary. Much of our culture is based on language. Any people who are aware of and in control of their own cultural anchors will reproduce and contribute to the language in a developmental manner. Our language is our connector to each other. It is what our mothers, fathers, grand-parents, aunts, uncles, cousins, and friends understand and taught us. It is how we share our laughter (Moms Mabley, Redd Foxx, and Richard Pryor quickly come to mind). It is with language that we bring in our new-borns and send out those who have joined our ancestors.

To me, it was clear that languages that work are creative sounds and moving feet, are voices in different colors, are mixed rhythms, and the creating of new words and structures. W.E.B. DuBois, Sterling Brown, Robert Hayden, Margaret Walker and Gwendolyn Brooks all wrote in English within a hidden force and beauty. Black folks took the droppings of European language and created a literature, a memory.

To the degree that our liberation is connected to communication, it becomes a self-creating prophecy that one speaks as one is. DuBois understood this and for over seventy-four years led the way in what Bradford T. Stull describes as "emancipatory composition," words that liberated our spirit, body and soul—language that encouraged us to reach for the unimaginable.

Arnold Rampersad, in his critical and insightful biography, *The Art and Imagination of W.E.B. DuBois*, feels that DuBois' poetry more than any other of his creative productions reveals more of the soul and wakening spirit of the young DuBois. Dr. Rampersad writes:

> In the context of his life's achievement, DuBois' poetry is an invaluable source for his private thoughts; in the context of his turn from conservatism and scholarly distance to agitation and propaganda, the poems underscore the depth of his soul-searching and the dignity of his motives. He was groping toward a full acceptance of the changes overtaking his life, as the

values to which he had dedicated himself through years of systematic
education as student and professor
appeared to be in serious jeopardy. He
was not easily converted to the role of
propagandist or political agitator. His
formal education, his scholarship, his
reverence for reason, his elitism, his
shyness, his craving for respectability,
and his involuntary coldness and
severity in certain social situations, all
held him back from radical activism. It
was one thing to fight racism with
facts and scholarship from the shelter
of the university. It was quite another
for a man of his place and time to risk
jail, to walk barefoot in protest, or to
devote his hard-won education to
propagandistic journalism.

I share this liberation as well as this resolu-
tion. I, as a young student and beginning poet
had come to realize that the days are not long
enough for the work that needs to be completed
and DuBois left a shining legacy for me to build
upon.

There is no separation between my cultural
self and my political, and writer selves. I am one,

and I am clear-always open for new knowledge, ideas, and revelations, but firmly anchored and connected to the millions of African (Black) women and men that led the way for my enlightenment and normalcy and W.E.B. DuBois must be accorded credit and thanks for his major contributions. Those of us that understand this must be at the forefront of creating, producing, and building that which we are for and sharing such development with our families, extended families, community, and world. It is easy to be against any number of ideas and institutions. The larger task is to fight that which we consider incorrect and build that which we consider good, just, and correct.

DuBois believed that the role of Black artists and intellectuals was not only to understand the text, but to write their version of the story, to teach the young the positive objectives of life, and to be involved at a community level-where theory is often never tested-in making real and substantive, long-term change in the lives of those who are truly suffering. This is DuBois' legacy. He was born February 23, 1868 and died August 27, 1963 in Ghana, on the eve of the major direct action demonstration of that time, the historic march of the 1960s, The March on Washington. He is in many ways, along with A.

Philip Randolph, Martin Luther King Jr. and Marcus Garvey, one of the fathers of our modern movement for freedom and democracy.

Dr. DuBois' work was transforming; it was moral and ethical work. The monetary rewards were few. However, the love generated by the hope in the eyes of our children as a result of such work is for me the best payment. Through his work, I learned that we must give our children a fighting chance in a world that long ago counted them out, diminished their chances of success to below zero. To see the yeses in their eyes is also to hear the yeses in our own heartbeats. This is why the drum is our magical instrument; you cannot kill the beat of hungry hearts and through the hunger in the heart of W.E.B. DuBois we, African Americans and Black people worldwide, are in a better position at the dawn of this new century and millennium. His passing this way and the gigantic and honorable legacy he left for us to build upon remains for me the truest test for any Black artist or intellectual. The bar has been set. It is now up to us, his cultural sons and daughters, to continue in the tradition of DuBois and others and contribute to his powerful example.

Black Art Museums

I didn't visit an art museum until adulthood. I was slapped into dumbness by the images of Black inferiority. Art as I understood it was what children did with crayons and watercolors. Art was also bought from hardware or department stores, mainly landscapes to hang in living rooms. This was the 1950s and Black visual artists were not able to speak nationally as a major voice to their people in the loud and loving images of their and our souls. Henry Ossawa Tanner, Margaret Taylor Goss-Burroughs, Aaron Douglas, Elizabeth Catlett, Charles White, John Biggers, Samella Sanders Lewis, Archibald J. Motley, Jr., Romare Bearden and others were laying groundwork for the sixties, that loving, difficult and dangerous decade that would alter the world and the landscape of our future in America.

Ebony Museum of Negro History

I was slowly becoming more and more isolated until I found the Ebony Museum of Negro History (soon to become the DuSable Museum of African American History) on the south side of Chicago. The Saturday morning in June of 1962, I arrived there looking for content that would offset the madness of daily military life. I was received at the door by a middle aged white man. His eyes displayed a welcome that I had only experienced once before. I soon learned that he was Jewish and one of the founders of the museum. Eugene Feldman embraced Black history and culture as if it was his own. I was to learn that he left the South due to anti-Semitism. His association with the other founders, Margaret and Charlie Burroughs, was to be a life long mission, some would say duty. He quickly took me to the kitchen where Margaret Burroughs was working on a linoleum cut. She was then, as now, a world-class visual artist whose ideas about art, Black folks, education, economics, history, psychology, culture and just about everything else was light years ahead of most people, Black and white. She was the first Black woman I met with a natural hairstyle. Her standard of beauty would soon be that of many

Blacks in America. She took me in without question, and another education began.

Mr. Feldman and I became friends, and his love for Black people and our history allowed me for the second time in my young life to communicate uninhibited with a white man, be he Jewish. There was a genuine warmth about him that I had experienced with the Jewish man who had taught me how to play the trumpet. They both loved Black people and Black culture. It seemed to me that the culture of our people gave greater meaning to their lives also.

Charlie and Margaret Burroughs

Charlie Burroughs, Margaret's husband, had been reared in the USSR and spoke Russian fluently. The Burroughs had a major library in their home. The museum took up the first floor and basement and they lived on the second and third floors. Charlie Burroughs introduced me to Russian writers and the politics of the left. Our long discussions about Alexander Pushkin, Vladimir Mayakovsky, Anton Chekhov, Anna Anhmatova, Boris Pasternak, Fyodor Dostoevsky, Osip Mandelstam, Leo Tolstoy and Ivan Turgenev to name a few kept me intellectually alive, stimulated and questioning my own existence. Margaret introduced me to Black visual artists who were coloring the world in their own image. She was also one of the founders of the South Side Community Art Center, and her own work had been critically received. She spoke lovingly of Charles White, John Biggers, Aaron Douglas, Samella Lewis, Romare Bearden, Jacob Lawrence, Elizabeth Catlett, Roy De Carava, Lois Mailou Jones, Archibald J. Motley, Jr. and others. Charlie and Margaret Burroughs introduced me to the works of Karl Marx. I knew at the age of twenty I was receiving a first-class education that others could only wish for. Charlie Burroughs and I would clash—often because I had been influenced deeply by Black Nationalism. The work of Marcus Garvey had impressed me; however. it was the young prophet Malcolm X of the Nation of Islam who lit me and my generation up and prepared us for the fight to come. It would be the sixties that impacted and changed America and the world for the best and Malcolm X was not teeth-smiling, tap dancing, scratching his head or confused about the power and unique influence of white world nationalism. I was becoming a Malcolm man and the politics of the left, most certainly the idea that the white and Black poor and working classes were going to somehow rise up and overthrow the capitalist pigs, was at least to me a powerful illusion. I knew this from the many fights and the continuous struggles of Black workers in Detroit at the Ford and GM plants against other white workers.

Also, I was keenly aware of the many battles on the left fought by Robeson, DuBois and especially Richard Wright, who left the John Reed Club due to the un-democratic, anti-intellectual climate of a dictatorial governing leadership and a cultural directorate that wanted him to write and act a certain way. In 1961 I

acquired a copy of *The God That Failed*, edited by
Richard Crossman. This book was essential to my
political education because among many Black
intellectuals and a few artists Marx had become a
living secular God. Six intellectuals/artists, who
had been intimately involved with communist
and fellow travelers contributed essays on why
they chose to leave or distance themselves from
their former comrades. Among the essayists were
Andre' Gide, Ignazio Silone, Stephen Spender,
Arthur Koestler, Louis Fischer and Richard
Wright. Wright's essay is one of the longest in the
book, providing a detailed account of his hunger
for like minded and thirsting individuals who
believe in Black equality. The men and women of
the left, mostly white and many Jewish,
encouraged Wright to produce and publish in
their various publications of the left.

One of the men who Wright was researching
to write an account of his life in the Communist
Party was about to be put out of the party. The
man, Ross, a Southern Black, married to a white
Jewish woman with one child, had committed
the carnal sin of questioning some of the policy
of the Communist Party. Ross was slated for
expulsion from the party on the grounds that he
was "anti-leadership" and a member of the local
leadership wanted to know how Wright felt

about Ross, but what he really wanted to know was the nature of Wright's loyalty to the party. Ross was an intellectual, and respected men and women who questioned authority. Wright was impressed with Ross and watched his mal-treatment while questioning at the same time why he was in the party. Wright, in his essay, tries to come to some understanding of the Communist leadership:

> Ross, the accused, sat alone at a table in the front of the hall, his face distraught. I felt sorry for him; yet I could not escape feeling that he enjoyed this. For him, this was perhaps the highlight of an otherwise bleak existence. In trying to grasp why Communists hated intellectuals, my mind was led back again to the accounts I had read of the Russian Revolution. There had existed in Old Russia millions of poor, ignorant people who were exploited by a few educated, arrogant noblemen, and it became natural for the Russian Communists to associate betrayal with intellectualism. But there existed in the Western world an element that

baffled and frightened the Communist party: the prevalence of self-achieved literacy. Even a Negro, entrapped by ignorance and exploitation—as I had been—could, if he had the will and the love for it, learn to read and understand the world in which he lived. And it was these people that the Communists could not understand.

This was why I was feeling so uncomfortable with much of the literature of the left. I was beginning to think for myself and the little writing I was doing at that time required deep reflection, study and much questioning.

Malcolm X

Malcolm X was the first Black man who had a national reputation and following that I saw and heard speaking truth to his people and to power. Before I heard Malcolm X, I was literally suffocating in a room full of "white" air. Malcolm X helped to shape my young voice. His voice was the immediate call, an S.O.S. to young Black men and women who felt deeply that we needed a Black leader that would push our agenda via direct action rather than always reacting to white world supremacy. Malcolm X had the voice, the walk, the nerve, the right education, the debating skills, the street smarts, the moral high ground, and a deep sense of urgency that we were all drawn to. It was he, his activism and unique organizing skills that truly nationalized The Nation of Islam. Above all, Malcolm X was perceived to be incorruptible. His private and public lives were not a contradiction. For young people like me, he was the perfect example of what a true revolutionary character should be. His ascetic lifestyle appealed to me. The major reservation I had was his religious affiliation. I had read enough history to know that the men of Islam were some of the first to enslave African people and colonize Africa. Their relationship to

African people was just as damaging as that of Christians. And I was not about to jump out of the earthquake into a volcano no matter how appealing brother Malcolm X was.

The words I would use to capture the essence of Malcolm X are integrity, dedication and quick study. Even when he was incorrect I believed he believed. His growth line is what impressed me the most. In between my debates and arguments with Charles Burroughs and listening to Malcolm X and deeply reflecting upon the books I was reading, I discovered the uniqueness and importance of culture. I now understood why Africa and African people were marginalized and diminished in the eyes of the world. Fundamentally, I learned that a person's contribution to society is closely related to his or her understanding and perception of himself or herself in relation to the culture in which he or she functions and lives. Such a culture can be one that either enslaves and shortens life or one that liberates and gives life. The best protection for any people can be found in culture that is intellectually and psychologically liberating. A liberation culture should be about the development of whole persons, and should begin that wholeness with an accurate assessment of a peoples' own involvement in their community, city, state, nation, and world.

For example, the normalization of Malcolm X, psychologically and intellectually, came about when he was a young man locked up in prison. I say that Malcolm X was normalized rather than radicalized because he was introduced to ideas that challenged and liberated his mind, ideas that put his people close to the center of civilization. He saw in the teachings of Elijah Muhammad and others a self-protective shield as well as the core wisdom for the making of a new Black person in America. From that point on, Malcolm X prepared himself to go on the offensive, to be proactive and combative in a self-reliant and self-protective manner. Any person, from any culture, functioning sanely would have acted the same way.

Continuing Education

My own development, or should I say mis-development, was not unlike that of millions of Black people in America. I was born into acute poverty, educated in public schools by insensitive and uncaring teachers, and dependent upon a welfare system that was demeaning, inadequate, and corrupt. I was nurtured in a single-parent family where my mother was ill-equipped to navigate the economic, social, and political pressures of our world. All of this drove her to alcohol, drugs, and death at the age of thirty five. My own transformation came about as a direct result of being introduced to African (Black) ideas that did not insult my own personhood, but guided me, invigorated me, and lifted me beyond the white supremacist theories that confined me and my people to the toilets of other people's promises and progress.

Yes, these ideas came fast and fresh in the forms of music and literature. Which, for me, confirmed the critical and affirming powers of Art. Art is fundamental instruction and intellectual food for a people's soul as they translate the many languages and acts of becoming whole and productive. Art at its best encourages us to walk on water, dance on top of trees and skip from star to star without being able to swim, skip a beat or fly.

All education must lead to deep understanding and mastery. The crucial question is, deep understanding and mastery of what? Introduction to many forms of knowing is absolutely necessary. However, most of the understandings about life that had been formerly taught to me had ceased to be life-giving and life-sustaining and did not lend themselves to self-reliance or deep reflection on the state of myself, or my family in this highly charged, competitive, and often oppressive world. I began to realize that one must be anchored in one's self, people, history, i.e. culture, before one can truly be a whole participant in world culture or multi-culturalism; we must always start local in order to appreciate and incorporate the positive agents of the universal. One cannot achieve the multi-anything if one has not explored the singular inside one's self. If a person doesn't start with the self first, odds are that he or she will end up confused and disliking his or her own Black, beige, brown or yellow skin.

In one of my early poems I tried to write about the doubleness of color and consciousness:

The Self-Hatred of Don L. Lee
(9/22/63)

i,
at one time,
loved
my
color—
it
opened sMall
doors of
tokenism
& acceptance.

(doors called, "the only one" &
"our negro")

after painfully
struggling
thru DuBois,
Rogers, Locke,
Wright & others,
my blindness
was vanquished
by pitchblack
paragraphs of
"us, we, me, i"
awareness.

i
began
to love
only a
part of
me—
my inner
self which
is all
black—
& developed a
vehement
hatred of
my light
brown
outer.

Epilogue

I am not a victim, I am not a left foot following nowhere or a loud lip spitting empty promises to undeveloped selves. I am not the missing seed in the garden of potential. I am not the race question or the undecided nod on a vacant head or disposable garbage looking for a landfill in crowded and poor neighborhoods.

I am a story, a long involved and on-going history. Often told orally in song, prose and verse, but not widely circulated in the pages of the best read newspapers, magazines, journals or books. I am the notes in the music you love. The nerve endings in your over used feet, the recently discovered gene that maps the genius of your foreparents. I am the yes hiding among the many no's of your fighting life. I am love and companion, warrior and clean fire, I always hear the cries of innocent children of all cultures and I wish to be able to respond with kindness, resources, truth-answers and a quality future where they, without hesitation, call my name.

My birth name is not my name. That name is not built upon a tradition of hardy fulfillment, deep accomplishments, readable history or bonding habits or traditions. That name is not farmers, wise markers or doers; not industrialists, scholars or flower designers. My birth name did not come from scientists or profound thinkers giving me a name to live up to. My birth name was not one that inspired greatness or near greatness. There was no discussion, no pre-planning, no anticipation, no curves in the rivers of Arkansas or cornbread crumbs on the concrete of Little Rock.

There was not, as in African tradition, a ceremony to name me. Nothing special, just a yellowblack baby named Don Luther Lee. Yellow but Black, the color that would determine much of my life. The Black, or African American community, is today more color and hair conscious than class conscious. White supremacist culture infected the very idea of America and its fundamental and guiding principle of "white is right, best and the future" is still with us and winning. Race remains the most destructive of America's realities. White remains the gold standard and the Blacker one is in color and most certainly in conversation and consciousness, the greater the chances that he or she will remain in the basement harvesting pennies and nickels, rather than enjoying the vast riches and promises of this conquered land. Few Americans, even the most educated, are aware that this country was built upon the bones and grounds of indigenous people, renamed Indians.

The first piece of writing I ever published dealt with this very delicate subject: I was born into slavery in February of 1942. In the spring of that same year 110,000 persons of Japanese descent were placed in protective custody by the white people of the United States. Two out of every three of these were American citizens by birth; the other third were aliens forbidden by law to be citizens. No charges had been filed against these people nor had any hearing been held. The removal of these people was on racial or ancestral grounds only. World War II, the war against racism; yet no Germans or other enemy aliens were placed in protective custody. There should have been Japanese writers directing their writings toward Japanese audiences.

Black. Poet. Black poet am I. This should leave little doubt in the minds of anyone as to which is first. Black art is created from black forces that live within the body. These forces can be lost at any time as in the case of The Black Bourgeoisie. Direct and meaningful contact with black people will act as energizers for the black forces. Black art will elevate and enlighten our people and lead them toward an awareness of self, i.e., their blackness. It will show them mirrors. Beautiful symbols. And will aid in the destruction of anything nasty and detrimental to our advancement as a people. Black art is a reciprocal art. The black writer learns from his people and because of his insight and "know how" he is able to give back his knowledge to the people in a manner in which they can identify, learn and gain some type of mental satisfaction, e.g., rage or happiness. We must destroy Faulkner, dick, jane and other perpetuators of evil. It's time for DuBois, Nat Turner and Kwame Nkrumah. As Frantz Fanon points out, "destroy the culture and you destroy the people." This must not happen. Black artists are culture stabilizers; bring back old values, and introduce new ones. Black art will talk to the people and with the will of the people stop the impending "protective custody."

America calling.
negroes.
can you dance?
play foot/baseball?
nanny?
cook?
needed now. negroes
who can entertain
ONLY.
others not
wanted.
(& are considered extremely dangerous.)

The politics of skin color in America is like an unlit match in the wooded northwest in 120 degree heat. The blacker one is the greater the odds of bush fires in his or her life. We are all taught from birth—formally and informally—that the lighter one is the better; it is a world phenomenon. I have witnessed it in India, Africa, Europe, South America and all the states of this nation. The devil's mark for my mother, sister and me was to be Yellowblack and, to compound our existence a hundred fold, we were urban poor and insufficiently educated, which brings me to the frequent quote of Dr. Carter G. Woodson from his *Mis-Education of the Negro*:

> When you control a man's thinking you do not have to worry about his actions. You do not have to tell him not to stand here or go yonder. He will find his "proper place" and will stay in it. You do not need to send him to the back door. He will go without being told. In fact, if there is no back door, he will cut one out for his special benefit. His education makes it necessary.

I do not know my father's unwritten history, I only know what he didn't give me. I still

became a responsible adult. I do know that he
died alone and was cremated without me and my
sister there to lie about his accomplishments. I
only knew my mother for seventeen years. My
sister, eight times prettier than I and a year and a
half younger, was always ahead of me socially.
Good looks in girls and women in a world of
ugly, hungry and angry men have a way of
determining their destiny before they understand
the power of their own magic. Jean Toomer
taught me this and Gwendolyn Brooks and Zora
Neale Hurston confirmed it. After absorbing
their work and that of other writers, I began to
understand why we were so poor, why my
mother died so young, and why my sister was
pre-destined for a life of early pleasure, dead-end
joy, debilitating ignorance, many children, many
men (seed donors—no fathers) physical and
emotional abuse and early aging. She did not
understand that: it is the sentencing of ideas that
cross borders. Finding it is not the challenge,
locating protein in ketchup or potato chips is not
a serious question in a nation of fat people who
elevate dieting to the status of a religion.
Crossing international borders via the internet is
no longer a mystery.

Few understand the acute failure of democratic capitalism and the ten commandments. In the four corners of the world, currency exchanges and pawn shops replace banks and credit unions. Mega churches, temples and mosques replace a caring creator whose only demand is good works, caring, quality sharing and service, love for the earth and its people. We have been ambushed by compassionate greed and deal makers eagerly demanding government bailouts for failed flight plans and bogus contracts. These are the urgent reasons for skydiving, speed learning, institution creation and indigenous cultures that encourage walking, reading, thinking, yoga, writing, research, meditation, and a serious work ethic, all seeking expert status in community wealth development and number crunching. Fore-shadowing a bold offensive in a world not ready for dark geniuses, who are highly motivated and more desirable and reliable than depending upon ignorant people talking about how ignorant other people are.

The biology of my family had already given me walking notice and declared me alien. My parental influences were no longer the people that gave me life, but were now books, music, and visual arts. I was alone on a highway going toward undefined battles. I did not, at the time, understand my role in the coming cultural wars. All I knew for certain was that Black literature, music and visual arts would be intricate in my maturation.

I had no idea at the time that Dudley Randall, poet and publisher of Broadside Press; Hoyt W. Fuller, editor of the Johnson publication *Negro Digest*; Barbara A. Sizemore, educator extraordinaire; Gwendolyn Brooks, poet and first Black to win a Pulitzer Prize; and Carol D. Easton, a brilliant thinker, educator, activist (and my future wife) would all impact my life like ocean water hitting a live volcano.

I did not realize at twenty-one that I was running on the same track as LeRoi Jones, soon to be Amiri Baraka and that he and the Black Arts Movement would help to define my mission in life. It was this movement—its intellectual center; its passionate hunger for liberation and justice; its bonding of us to Africa, Africans and the best they had to offer; its rallying cry for independence, self-defense and self-reliance— that became my life's work. It was this movement that demanded integrity and authenticity and eventually would give me a new name, Haki R. Madhubuti.

However, it would be poetry—the defining language of all cultures—that would capture my being like a junkie to drugs. I read and wrote poetry as if it was my breakfast, lunch and dinner. Black poetry fed my need for meaning and confirmed in me that literature, and that art, can transform a life. It worked on me. Everything I would do or become is because of poetry. That I would meet and interact with most of the major Black poets and writers of the twentieth century and also be intimately involved with the major human rights struggles of Black people would be the fuel for volume two of my memoirs on my life.